Openings in History

Series Editor: Robert Unwin

Saxon and Viking Britain

Peter Wenham

Hutchinson
London Melbourne Sydney Auckland Johannesburg

Hutchinson Education

An imprint of Century Hutchinson Ltd

62-65 Chandos Place, London WC2N 4NW

Century Hutchinson Australia Pty Ltd
PO Box 496, 16-22 Church Street, Hawthorn, Victoria 3122, Australia

Century Hutchinson New Zealand Ltd
PO Box 40-086, Glenfield, Auckland 10, New Zealand

Century Hutchinson South Africa (Pty) Ltd
PO Box 337, Bergvlei 2012, South Africa

First published 1980
Reprinted 1981, 1982, 1983, 1984, 1987

Set in IBM Univers and Century by Tek-Art Ltd

Printed and bound in Great Britain by
Anchor Brendon Ltd, Tiptree, Essex

British Library Cataloguing in Publication Data
Wenham, Peter
    Saxon and Viking Britain.—(Openings in history
    series; vol. 2)
    1. Great Britain—History—To 1066—Juvenile
    literature
    I. Title II. Series
    941.01   DA135

ISBN 0 09 138551 2

Contents

1 The Angles and Saxons land

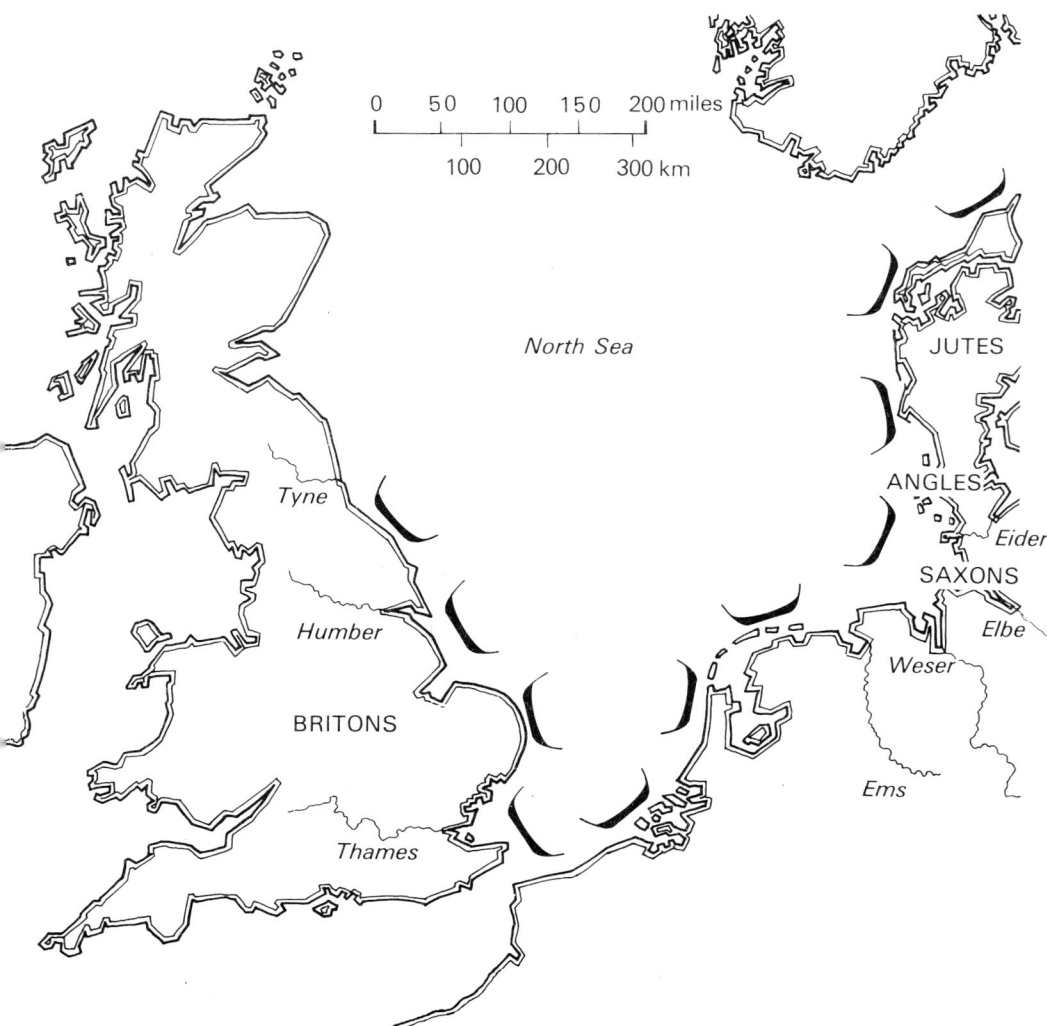

A modern sketch map showing the invasion of Britain by the Anglo-Saxons, which began during the fourth century AD

Away she went over a wavy
ocean
boat like a bird, breasting
seas . . . .
Till the curved prow had
ploughed so far . . .
that they might see land
loom on the skyline,
then the shimmer of the
cliffs . . . .

An extract from an Anglo-Saxon poem which describes a voyage of the hero Beowulf

1 Name the sea and the main rivers which the Angles and Saxons navigated.

2 Use the scale on the map to work out the distance the Angles and Saxons sailed across the North Sea to the coast of Britain.

3 The poem *Beowulf* makes the sea voyage sound swift and exciting. Do you think voyages were always like that? Give your reasons.

The invasions

The Angles and the Saxons were driven from their own country by tribes from the east, and were forced to seek new land. They were a seafaring people and began to cross the sea to explore Britain. At first they came in small raiding parties of warriors, plundering and then returning home. Britain was not well defended, mainly because the Britons were ruled by tribal chiefs who quarrelled among themselves. We can still read what the invasion might have been like from a Saxon poem called *Beowulf*. The Saxons loved story-telling, and this adventure is about a legendary warrior and seaman with the name of Beowulf.

The first settlements

Because their ships were small, the Angles and Saxons had to make many journeys. In fact, the invasions went on for 150 years. When they arrived on the shores of Britain, they rowed up the rivers. They passed swamps and densely wooded banks until they reached a place where a clearing could be made and wooden huts built. The early settlements were small and usually started in valleys where the soil was rich. Gradually groups of Anglo-Saxons moved further inland in search of farming land.

4 Look at the artist's picture below and say how the Anglo-Saxons powered their ships.
5 How was the ship steered?
6 How do you think the Britons felt when they saw the Anglo-Saxon warship with its carved wooden head being rowed into shore?
7 Design a carved wooden head for a Saxon ship and make a sketch of it.
8 Where did the Anglo-Saxons make their settlements? What happened to the Britons?
9 Find out all you can from books about the stories of King Arthur and the Knights of the Round Table.

This Saxon warboat was put together from remains which were found in a marsh in Germany. It is a light, open craft, built of oak, and measures 22.84 metres long and only 3.26 metres wide. It was rowed by 36 oarsmen and could hold 45 people altogether

A carved wooden head like this often decorated the front of the ship

The Britons

As the Saxons made their way into new areas, small battles had to be fought, which the newcomers generally won. However, at one time there seems to have been strong resistance to the invaders. Legends tell of a war leader called King Arthur who with his army won great victories over the Anglo-Saxons. Eventually most of the British tribes fled from their lands to the mountains of the north and west. Those who remained either became slaves or continued to live on their farms on the hills while the invaders kept to the valleys.

An artist's impression of an Anglo-Saxon boat approaching Britain

2 Saxon houses

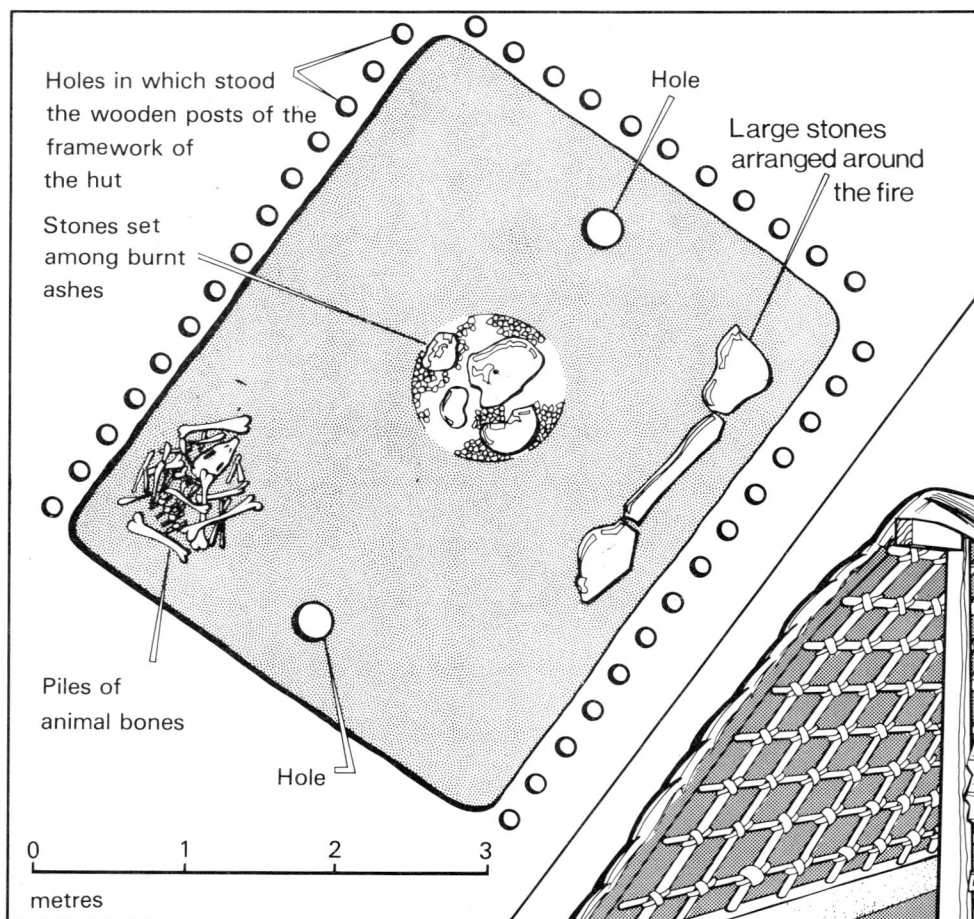

Holes in which stood
the wooden posts of the
framework of
the hut

Stones set
among burnt
ashes

Hole

Large stones
arranged around
the fire

Piles of
animal bones

Hole

0   1   2   3

metres

The plan of a Saxon hut was drawn during an excavation in Gloucestershire

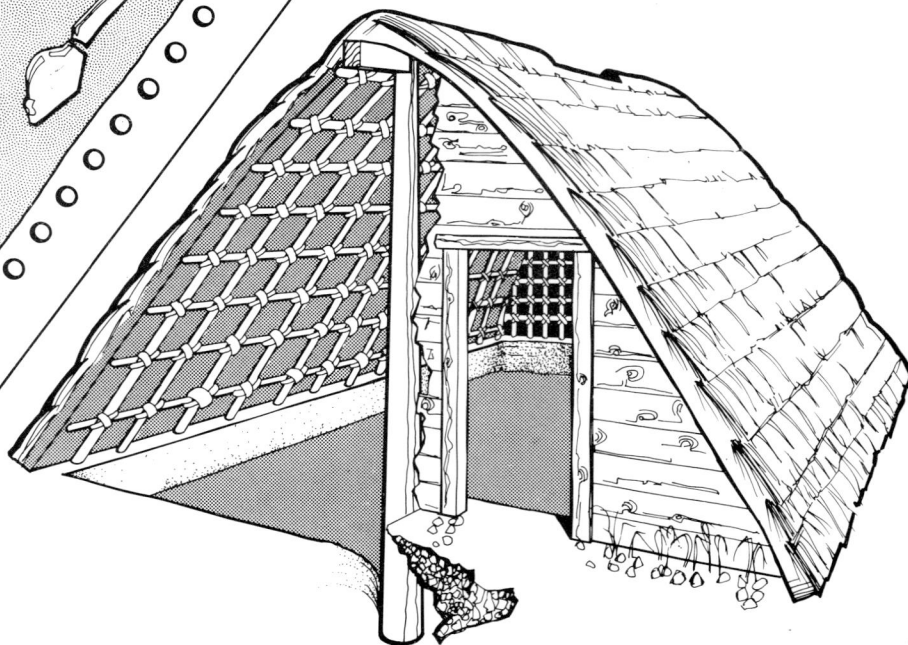

The reconstruction drawing shows what the hut looked like in Saxon times

The Saxon hut

When a group of Saxons had chosen a place to settle, the first task was to cut down the trees with axes and build homes. Houses were made of wood and were built near to each other. They varied in size, from small huts like the one above to much larger buildings. It was easy to see how important a person was by the size of house he owned. However, most houses were built in the same way. First a strong framework of timber beams was erected, then the walls were filled in with intertwined twigs and covered with clay.

The roof was sharply pointed, and made of wooden beams, thatched with turf or reeds. Sometimes the roof sloped right down to the ground, and the Saxons dug out the soil inside the hut to a depth of about two feet so that the roof rested on low earth walls. Saxon huts provided one main room in which the family lived, ate and slept. Food was cooked on the hearth fire in clay pots, and at night straw-filled pillows and animal skins were spread out to sleep on. There were no windows, so smoke from the hearth escaped through a hole in the roof.

A Saxon lord and lady eating and drinking at table with their guests

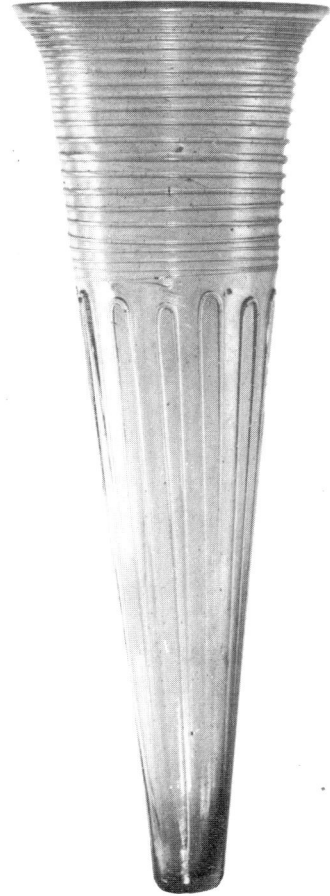

A glass tumbler of the kind you can see in the picture of the feast. It was held in the hand until empty, then turned upside-down on the table

1 What was the size of the hut?
2 What do the burnt ashes on the excavation plan indicate?
3 Why were the stones found placed among the burnt material?
4 Use the excavation plan and the picture of the reconstructed hut to say what stood in the two holes inside the hut.
5 What do you think the large stones were used for?
6 Make a list of the objects on the Saxon table.
7 Explain how you think a 'tumbler' got its name.
8 Imagine you are a slave at a Saxon feast. Describe what you do, see and hear.

The lord's Hall

The lord of the village had the largest house, called a Hall. It was surrounded by a number of smaller buildings, called 'bowers'. These were used as bedrooms for the lord and his family, kitchens, workshops and sleeping quarters for slaves. A mound of earth with a fence on top surrounded the Hall and its adjoining huts so that they were protected in time of war. Inside the Hall, the earth floor was covered with rushes, which were changed when they become soiled. The walls were often covered with tapestries and hung with shields and weapons.

Long tables and benches lined the walls of the Hall. They were used for eating, and then at night were strewn with mattresses for the lord's warriors to sleep on. Saxon lords enjoyed feasting. The lord, lady and their guests sat at a long table across the top of the Hall, while the warriors sat down the sides. Slaves served the meals. Boiled meat, roasted joints and loaves of bread were the usual foods, and plenty of ale and mead (a drink made from honey) was drunk. After the feast minstrels sang songs about gods and great heroes.

3 People in the village

These two scenes from an Anglo-Saxon calendar show (above)
a lord hawking and (below) shepherds at work

Different kinds of people

The Saxons in the village belonged to different social classes. The 'eorl' or lord was the most important man. He owned large estates and had slaves to do the work. Next to him in rank was the 'ceorl' or freeman. He either owned his land or rented land from the lord. Below him came the half-free man, who had only a very small amount of land and had to work for the lord for part of the week. The poorest man of all was the slave, who belonged to his master and was fed and clothed in return for his work.

Work

Everyone had different duties. The lord went armed to help the king in times of danger. At home the lord not only kept his large household in order, but also settled disputes between villagers. However, he did have time for his favourite pastimes of hawking and hunting. Most freemen spent their days farming, but some followed other trades and occupations. There was work for potters, smiths, carpenters, shoewrights, bakers and many others. Slaves held less skilled jobs like bee-keeping, herding

The front panel of a carved whalebone box found in Northumbria, dating from about AD 700

1 In the hawking picture which man is the servant and which is the lord?
2 Describe what the two shepherds are doing.
3 List as many reasons as you can to show why the Saxon lord was a very important man.
4 How many men and women are shown in the carving?
5 What differences are there between men's and women's clothes?
6 Describe in detail the artist's drawing of the clothes worn by a Saxon farmer.
7 Make a chart showing the order of importance of the various kinds of people in the Saxon village, and draw a sketch of each.

A modern drawing of a Saxon farmer

sheep and making cheese. Women did brewing, spinning and weaving as well as looking after their families and working in the fields.

Clothes

Style of dress was much the same for everyone though the poor dressed in rough material, while the wealthy wore fine wool and linen garments. Men's clothing can be seen in the drawing opposite. Women had tunics down to their feet with loose sleeves. They wore hoods on their heads and cloaks to give extra warmth. Both men and women fastened their clothing with brooches and buckles. The clothes of the rich were often dyed with bright colours. A Saxon historian, Bede (see Opening 12), wrote that the scarlet dye made from shellfish was 'a most beautiful colour which never fades with the heat of the sun or the washing of the rain'.

4 Farming

This farming scene, and the two opposite, are monthly pictures from an Anglo-Saxon calendar. This picture shows ploughing in January

1 What animals were used to pull the plough?
2 Explain what the men at the front and rear of the plough teams are doing.
3 Imagine you are an Anglo-Saxon farmer. Write a brief account saying whether or not you think the open field system is a fair one.

This photograph shows large open fields divided into strips. Each strip took one day to plough

New farming methods

The Anglo-Saxons brought a new kind of farming. With their heavy ploughs they broke up the clay soil in the valleys. It was hard work, but gradually many parts of the country were cultivated for the first time. Previously the Britons, because of their inferior ploughs, had only worked the light soils of the hilly regions. The people in each village ploughed enough land to produce sufficient crops to feed themselves. Unlike the Britons, who had small fields, they began to divide the land into two, three or four huge fields, which were called 'open' fields because they had no permanent fencing.

Open fields

These large fields were split up into strips which were shared out between families. Each farmer's strips were scattered about over the fields so that everyone had a share of good and bad, near and distant land. Although each farmer cultivated his own strips, they all joined together to help at harvest time. The strips were ploughed with teams of oxen. Because it was difficult turning the team round, the length of the strip was limited to the amount of land the oxen could cover without stopping to rest. The team was turned round upon the headland at the edge of the field before starting the next furrow.

Digging the soil and sowing seed in March

Hay-making in June

4 Make a list of, and describe, the tools that the men are using in the pictures above.

5 Use the three pictures from the Anglo-Saxon calendar to say what the main differences are between Saxon farming and farming today.

6 Complete the chart below to show what the Saxons used animals for:

Animals	Uses
pigs	meat, skin
sheep	
cattle	
oxen	

Crops

Every year, one of the fields in turn was left fallow. No crops were grown in it, but animals were allowed to graze there so that they would manure it. The other fields were cultivated. The chief crops — wheat, rye and barley — were used for making coarse bread, and barley also provided malt for brewing ale. Peas and beans were grown too, as well as flax for making linen clothes. In addition to their strips, most families had a small plot in which they grew vegetables such as cabbages, onions and marrows. Herbs were grown for seasoning in cooking and for making medicines.

Animals

Rearing animals was also important. Pigs roamed through the forest, while sheep and cattle grazed near the village on meadows and wasteland. Meadows were fenced and shared out each year. Each farmer jealously guarded his right to pasture his cattle and collect his hay. The amount of hay produced was only enough for a few animals to be fed through the winter. So in autumn many beasts were slaughtered, and the meat salted to preserve it. Cattle also provided milk, butter and cheese; the sheep gave wool; and the horns of oxen were used for drinking horns and their hides for leather.

5 Saxon crafts

A simple clay cooking pot

A funeral urn in which the ashes of a cremated body were placed

A purse lid decorated with gold, garnets and coloured glass, found in the Sutton Hoo ship burial (see Opening 6)

1 What do you notice about the markings on the funeral urn?
2 List the differences between the two pots.
3 Explain how the way the Saxons buried their dead has helped us to know about their crafts.
4 Make a Saxon pot with either plasticine or clay.
5 Describe the decorations on the purse lid.

We have evidence of the craftsmanship of the Anglo-Saxons from several kinds of objects which have survived till today.

Grave goods

First are the funeral urns in which the Saxons put the ashes of their dead. Later, they buried their dead rather than cremating them. Other objects have been found in graves. It was the custom, before the Saxons became Christians, to lay personal belongings in the grave. It was believed that the dead would need them in the after-life. For example, among the contents of the grave of a Saxon chieftain at Taplow in Buckinghamshire were a spear, a sword, two shields, a knife, a ring, a bucket, a bronze bowl, glass cups, drinking horns and thirty bone chessmen.

Other crafts

Most is known about the work of the potter, the glassmaker and the metalworker. The simplest pots were the plain cooking utensils, some of which were handmade by the women of the village. As time went on, potters became more skilled and produced a variety of shapes — bowls, jugs with spouts and handles, and storage jars up to nearly one metre high. The most elaborately

This silver brooch made in the ninth century is 11.5 centimetres in diameter

A smith beating out metal

6 The silver brooch contains five figures in the centre representing the five senses (sight, taste, hearing, smell and touch). Complete the following chart.

Sense	Position on the brooch
sight	centre
	top left
	top right
	bottom left
	bottom right

7 Why do you think wealthy Saxons liked to own jewellery? Do people today wear jewellery for the same reasons?

8 Imagine you are a Saxon metalworker. Design a brooch for either your lord or his lady.

decorated pots were funeral urns. Saxon glassware was also made in many different forms and was attractively coloured with yellows, greens, browns and blues. The workmanship of Saxon metalworkers is still much admired today.

Jewellery

Wealthy men and women in Anglo-Saxon times greatly enjoyed wearing jewellery. Brooches were made from gold, silver and bronze and were used for fastening cloaks and gowns. They came in various shapes and were frequently richly decorated. Often birds and animals were represented in elaborate twisting designs. Men liked to wear large ornamental buckles on their belts and seemed to enjoy wearing rings as much as women did. A rich lady usually wore a great deal of jewellery. Her hair might be done up with a jewelled band, her arms adorned with bangles, while a necklace of gold, amethyst or even glass beads might hang about her neck.

6 The Sutton Hoo ship burial

The lords of the people then built
a mound on the headland; it was high and
                                    broad
and could be seen from far out at sea.
In ten days they built the monument
for that hero . . . .
They put in it rings and jewellery . . . .
The whole of his treasure they put in the
                                    ground,
where it lies to this day. . . .
Then round the grave mound rode the
                                    warriors . . .
mourning their ruler . . . and loudly praising
all his brave deeds.

A passage from the Saxon poem Beowulf, *written in the eighth century, which describes the burial of a king*

1   Explain what you can see in the photograph of the excavation.
2   Why did the people build a 'monument' for their ruler?
3   Imagine you were present at the funeral ceremony at Sutton Hoo. Write a description or make a strip cartoon to tell everything that happened, e.g. preparing the trench, dragging the ship from the river and placing the treasure in the ship.

A photograph taken during the excavation at Sutton Hoo

Excavating the mound

One of the most exciting excavations in Britain was concerned with the Anglo-Saxons. In 1938 some archaeologists became interested in a group of eleven mounds near a river about six miles from the sea in Suffolk. The place was called Sutton Hoo. In the following year, the largest mound, which was oval in shape, was opened up. As the sandy soil was dug away, the shape of a boat began to appear. Although the timbers had rotted away, the sand was darker where they had been. Guided by the different coloured soil and the iron nails that still remained, the archaeologists were able to lay bare the complete outline of a Saxon ship. The ship had no mast or sail, but would have been rowed by thirty-eight oarsmen. It was 27 metres long and 4½ metres wide. On the bottom of the ship, in the centre, were the remains of a specially built burial chamber. It had collapsed with the weight of earth piled up on top. Inside it, caked with soil, was the richest hoard of Saxon funeral treasure that had ever been found in Europe. Chemical tests showed there might have been a human body in the chamber, but there was no visible proof.

A stone sceptre, 82 centimetres long, with carved faces and painted knobs in a bronze casing

4 Describe the helmet.
5 In whose honour do you think this grave was built? Give reasons for your answer.
6 Imagine you were one of the archaeologists working at Sutton Hoo. Describe what you saw and how you felt when the treasure was discovered.

A helmet, decorated with bronze, silver and garnets

The blade of the sword has rusted into the leather scabbard; the hilt is gold and jewelled

Burial customs

Nobody is sure whether a body or the ashes from a cremation were ever buried in this large grave. Archaeologists think that it was probably a memorial to a great man who perhaps died fighting in battle during the seventh century and whose body was never recovered. In his honour, the ship was dragged half a mile up from the river and laid in a trench. After the possessions of the dead man had been placed in it, earth was piled on top to mark the place. This was a custom with the graves of rich people. Archaeologists can try to work out whose grave it might have been by considering the objects buried with the ship.

The treasure

There were several objects in the ship. In addition to helmets and swords, other weapons found were spears and a throwing-axe, together with a coat of mail and a large round shield decorated with bird and dragon figures. Gleaming silverware was dug out — silver drinking horns, bowls, and spoons — but the most magnificent finds were the pieces of jewellery. There were buckles, clasps and buttons, all of gold, most richly decorated and set with jewels. Two unusual objects were also discovered: an ornate iron standard 170 centimetres high and a carved sceptre which might have belonged to a king.

7 Anglo-Saxon place-names

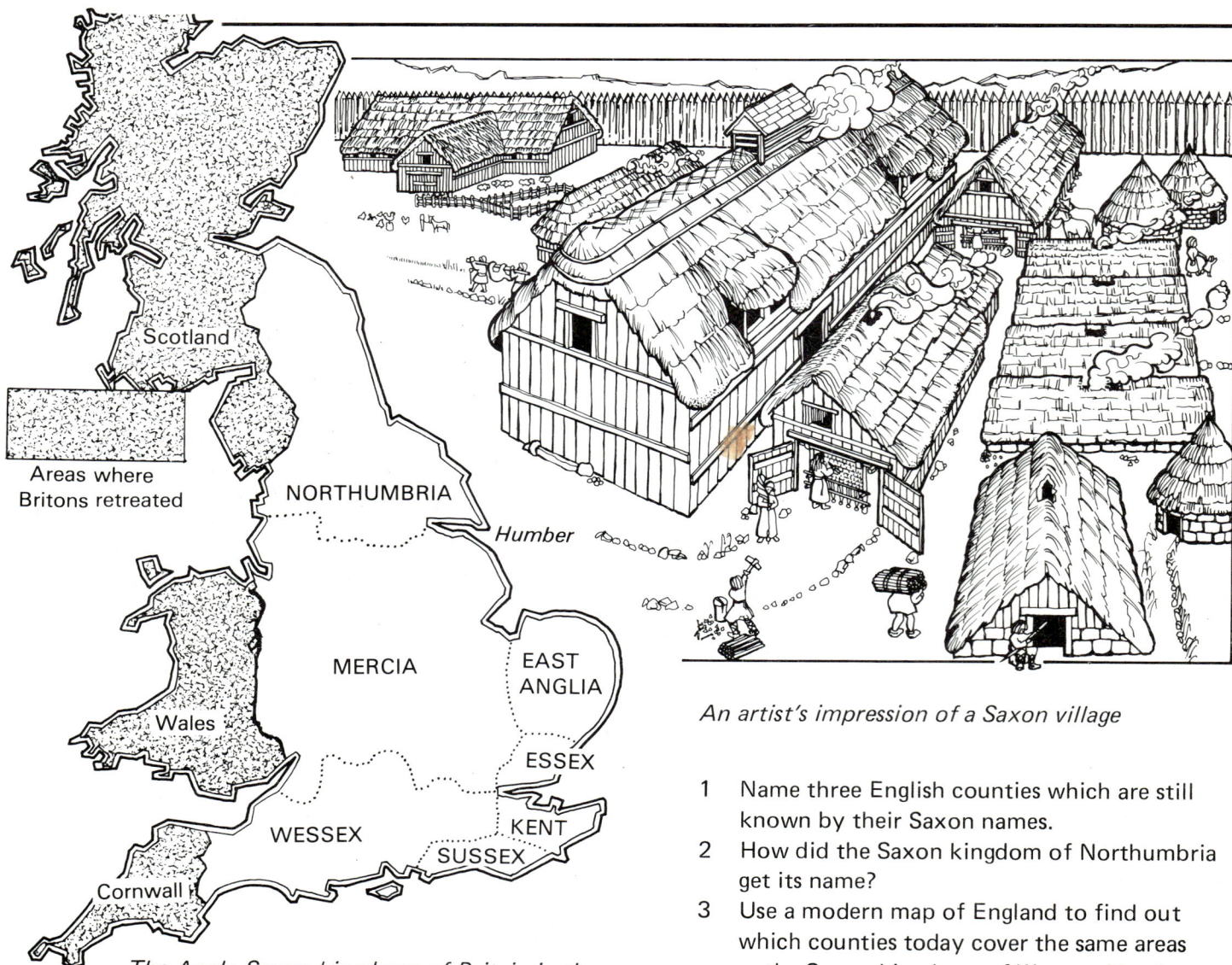

The Anglo-Saxon kingdoms of Britain in the seventh century

An artist's impression of a Saxon village

1 Name three English counties which are still known by their Saxon names.
2 How did the Saxon kingdom of Northumbria get its name?
3 Use a modern map of England to find out which counties today cover the same areas as the Saxon kingdoms of Wessex, Mercia and Northumbria.

Studying place-names

Various types of evidence from the past, like documents and objects dug up by archaeologists, tell us about the people in history. Another kind of evidence is place-names. The Anglo-Saxons who came to Britain gave names to the places where they settled. Many of these names are still used today. Most important of all, it was the Angles who gave their name to England (Angle-land). A study of place-names shows how modern names have developed and proves how lasting the language of the Angles and Saxons has been.

Names of counties

The Anglo-Saxon invaders drove the Britons into the mountains and settled in the rest of the country. For a long time there was not just one Anglo-Saxon kingdom in England, but seven. Most of the names which the Anglo-Saxons gave to their kingdoms are still in use, for example Essex, the home of the East Saxons. However, there are some names, such as Wessex, that are no longer used. The kingdom of East Anglia was divided into two: the people who lived in the north (the north folk) gave Norfolk its name; those who lived in the south (the south folk) gave Suffolk its name.

Use the map, which shows the places containing the name '-ing' settled by the Angles and Saxons, and the information below to answer these questions.

4   In which parts of the country did the Anglo-Saxons mainly settle?

5   Work out the modern names of the following places settled by the Anglo-Saxons:
    — the place where the people and their chief Hasta lived
    — the homestead by the River Trent
    — the farm (or 'wick') that was well known for its butter
    — the hamlet (or 'ton') near a hill

6   How do you think the following places — Southampton, Darlington, Cottingham — got their names?

7   What clues do Anglo-Saxon place-names give about the main occupations and the lives of the people?

8   Find out as many Anglo-Saxon place-names as you can in the area in which you live and keep your eyes open for signposts when you go on journeys.

This map shows all the places with '-ing' in their names, which we can tell were settled by the Angles and the Saxons

---

Place-names

This is a list of the most common word endings used by the Angles and Saxons:

— ING meant the *people* of one large family or tribe
— TON meant a *farmstead* or *hamlet*
— HAM meant a *homestead*, often near a river
— FORD meant a *shallow part of a river* where it could be crossed
— BURY meant a *fortified place*
— WICK/WICH was another name for a *hamlet* or *farmstead*
— LEY/LEAGH meant a *clearing in a forest*
— HURST meant a *wood*

Places were often named after a *chief*:
— Reada was a chief, so the place where he and his people settled was called READING.
— Beorma was a chief of a group of people who made a homestead called BIRMINGHAM.

Places were also named after *local features*:
— CREDITON was the farm on the River Creedy.
— STAMFORD was the ford with the stony (stam) bottom.

Places were sometimes named after the *food* or *materials* that were produced there:
— WOOLWICH was the farm where much wool was produced.

8 The Celtic church

A Celtic cross, carved with complicated patterns, at Clonmacnois in Ireland

A cross from Ruthwell in Scotland, showing scenes from the life of Jesus

1 List the differences between the two crosses.
2 What was the purpose of showing scenes from the Bible on crosses?
3 Why were the crosses made of stone, rather than wood?

The early Celtic church

When the Saxons invaded Britain, they brought with them their religion. They worshipped gods of the earth, sea and sky. The king of the gods was Woden, the god of war was Tiw and Thunor was the god of thunder. Meanwhile in the mountains to which the Britons fled, the Christian religion grew in strength, especially in Wales. Because another name for the Britons was Celts, the church to which the British Christians belonged was called the Celtic church. St Patrick, who was born in Wales, became a missionary and travelled through Ireland between AD 432 and 461, preaching and setting up monasteries.

Monasteries

About one hundred years after Patrick's death, St Columba sailed from Ireland with twelve disciples to the lonely island of Iona, off the west coast of Scotland. Here he founded a monastery. As in most Celtic monasteries, the monks lived in separate cells built of stone and only met together to eat and pray. They wore simple woollen garments and led a hard life. Each monastery had its own rules and its own abbot was in charge. The monks were free to wander from one monastery to another. They often stopped at wooden crosses on the way, to preach to the people. Later, stone crosses were set up.

Two sites chosen by Celtic monks: Skellig Michael, off the south coast of Ireland, where cells were built in the rocks; and the island of Lindisfarne, linked to the mainland only at low tide, when a causeway of land is uncovered (above)

4 Describe the situations of the two monasteries. How would the monks have crossed to each?
5 Why do you think the monks chose Lindisfarne and Skellig Michael as the places to build their monasteries?
6 Draw a sketch map to show the spread of Celtic Christianity in Britain.
7 Find out from books as much as you can about the lives of St Patrick, St Columba and St Aidan.

Christianity reaches England

The monks travelled widely and preached with courage and enthusiasm. People were impressed by their learning and their saintly lives. From Iona monks spread a knowledge of Christianity down through the west of Scotland to the rest of the north of Britain. At first the monks preached to the Britons and did not attempt to convert the Saxon invaders. However, eventually Oswald, the Saxon king of Northumbria, invited missionaries from Iona to his kingdom. In AD 634 St Aidan arrived with a small band of monks and built a monastery on the island of Lindisfarne, just off the coast.

St Aidan

Aidan travelled on foot through Northumbria preaching Christianity. Until Aidan learned the language, the king himself went with him to act as interpreter. Aidan met all kinds of people, and soon became well loved. He refused all payment and gave away any gifts. When he was not teaching, he was reading and studying. More monks came from Iona and elsewhere in Scotland to help him preach, build churches and set up monasteries. During the next twenty years Christianity became firmly established in Northumbria. When Aidan died, his monks carried on his work south of Northumbria.

9 St Cuthbert

Cuthbert on Farne Island

A twelfth-century wall painting, thought to be of Cuthbert as a bishop, from Durham Cathedral

1 List the main differences between the pictures of Cuthbert on Farne Island and Cuthbert as a bishop.

2 Both pictures of Cuthbert date from the twelfth century. Can we be sure they are a true likeness of Cuthbert? Give reasons for your answer.

3 Explain why St Cuthbert, according to Bede, was a successful preacher.

The life of St Cuthbert

One of the best loved and most famous Christian leaders in Northumbria was Cuthbert, the shepherd boy who became a saint. Bede, also a monk (see Opening 12), wrote a history of Cuthbert's life, so we know a good deal about him. Cuthbert was born about AD 634. He worked as a shepherd until he was sixteen. He then became a monk. For many years Cuthbert travelled far and wide. Bede wrote: 'Cuthbert was so skilful a speaker and had such light in his angelic face and such love for proclaiming his message . . . . He became famous for his miracles and his prayers restored sufferers from all kinds of disease.'

Cuthbert on Farne Island

But Cuthbert longed to be able to pray in complete peace. In AD 676 he went to live as a hermit on Farne Island, cut off from the rest of the world. Bede tells us, 'Cuthbert was the first man brave enough to live [on Farne Island]. He served God in solitude for many years in a hut surrounded by a wall so high that he could see nothing but the heavens . . . so that eyes and thoughts might be kept from wandering and inspired to seek for higher things.' Cuthbert grew his own barley, and one famous story tells how the birds stopped stealing his crop when he asked them to go.

Monks opening Cuthbert's coffin at Lindisfarne

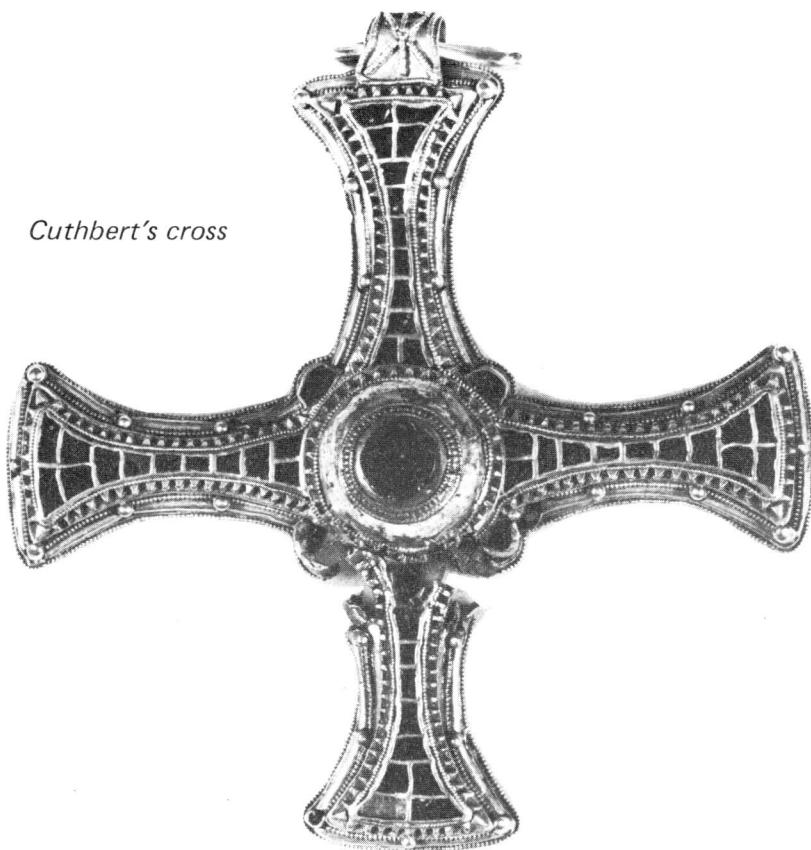

Cuthbert's cross

After eleven years they expected to find his flesh reduced to dust and the remains withered as is usual in dead bodies . . . . When the monks opened the grave they found the body whole as though still living . . . so that he looked as if he were asleep rather than dead. Furthermore all the vestments in which he was clothed appeared not only spotless but wonderfully fresh and fair.

A description of the scene from Bede's History of the English Church and People

4   Draw and colour Cuthbert's cross.

5   Can you see any damage on the cross? If so, explain.

6   Write a brief account of the opening of Cuthbert's coffin in AD 698 from the point of view of one of the monks at the ceremony.

7   Make a time chart listing the main events in St Cuthbert's life.

Cuthbert as bishop

Nine years later the king of Northumbria persuaded Cuthbert to leave his island and become Bishop of Lindisfarne. He travelled the countryside preaching for two years, but returned to Farne Island shortly before his death in AD 687.

Cuthbert was an inspiring person. He is famous for his teaching and his kindness to people and animals. He was a man of great energy and strength in spite of suffering from disease. He was also noted for his fasting and his penances. Bede wrote about his many miracles of healing. Cuthbert was made a saint.

Cuthbert's coffin

Cuthbert's corpse has had a strange history. Eleven years after Cuthbert's death, the monks at Lindisfarne opened up his grave in order to bury him more richly. His body was then put in a new coffin. In AD 875, afraid that the Vikings might destroy this coffin, the monks took it away from Lindisfarne. Eventually the coffin was carried for safe-keeping to Durham. Later the magnificent cathedral of Durham was built, largely in Cuthbert's honour. His coffin was opened in 1538. In 1827, when it was opened once again, his beautiful cross was found within the wrappings around his body.

10 The Roman church

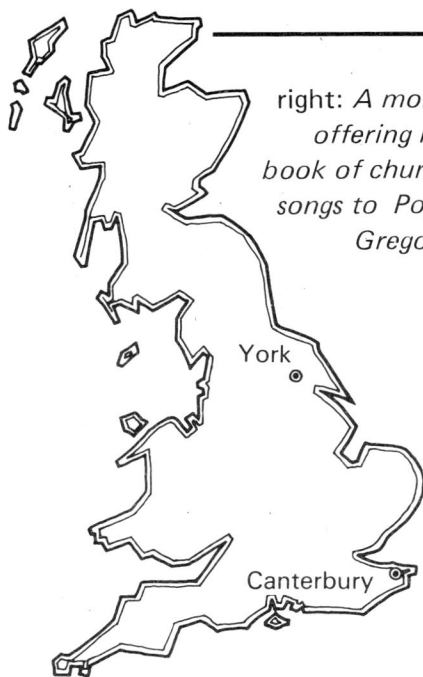

The two main centres of the Roman church in Britain

right: *A monk offering his book of church songs to Pope Gregory*

He tried to serve both Christ and the ancient gods and had in the same temple an altar to Christ side by side with an altar on which victims were offered to devils.

from Bede's History of the English Church and People, *Book 2, ch. 15*

1 How can you tell from the picture above that Gregory was an important churchman?
2 The quotation on the left describes the conversion of King Raedwald. How much influence had St Augustine achieved?
3 Draw a strip cartoon showing the main events of St Augustine's mission to England.

The mission of St Augustine: Canterbury

While St Columba (see Opening 8) was living his simple life on Iona, the Pope of the church in Rome, Gregory, was also thinking about converting the pagan English to Christianity. In AD 597 he sent Augustine with forty monks to England. They landed in the kingdom of Kent and were well received since King Ethelbert's wife, Bertha, was already a Christian. Nevertheless the king was suspicious of Augustine and insisted on meeting him in the open air where he believed he would be safer from his magic! Later, however, impressed by Augustine's preaching, the king invited him to Canterbury.

Augustine was given the use of Queen Bertha's small church. Soon the king was baptized and many of his subjects obediently followed his example. Pope Gregory made Augustine the first archbishop of the English church, and because Canterbury was King Ethelbert's chief city it became the archbishop's headquarters. King Saebert of Essex and King Raedwald of East Anglia also became Christians through Ethelbert's influence. However, most of the work of conversion was undone after the deaths of Augustine and the three Christian kings. The kings who followed were pagans, and only in Kent did Christianity survive at this time.

The pagan priest Coifi makes a decision

I have long realized that there was nothing in what we worshipped, for the more I sought after truth in our religion, the less I found. I now publicly confess that this teaching clearly reveals truths that will afford us the blessings of life, salvation and eternal happiness. Therefore, Your Majesty, I submit that the temples and altars that we have dedicated to no advantage be immediately desecrated and burned.

from Bede's History of the English Church and People, *Book 2, ch. 13*

The modern font which stands in the crypt of York Minster, on the exact spot where King Edwin is believed to have been baptized

4   The five figures on the panels above the font are St Paulinus, King Edwin, Queen Ethelberga, St Hilda of Whitby, and St James the Deacon. Work out who is who and list their names from left to right.

5   Why did Coifi, the priest, decide to change his religion?

6   Complete this chart:

	Date	Missionary	Kingdom	King	Queen
Canterbury					
York					

The mission of St Paulinus: York

In AD 625 the pagan King Edwin of Northumbria was to marry the Christian Ethelberga, daughter of King Ethelbert of Kent. Paulinus, one of Augustine's monks, travelled north with her and James the Deacon to spread Christianity. King Edwin listened to Paulinus but consulted his council before accepting the Christian faith. At this meeting the priest, Coifi, decided to abandon his old religion and become a Christian. He galloped on horseback to his pagan temple and threw a spear at it! Later the temple was destroyed.

King Edwin was baptized in a wooden church in York in AD 627, and during the same year many other people were converted. Paulinus would have become Archbishop of York but, as earlier in Kent, there was a setback for the Roman church. King Edwin was killed in battle in AD 633 by the pagan King Penda of Mercia. Paulinus fled with Queen Ethelberga back to Kent. It was St Aidan of the Celtic church (Opening 8) who, arriving a year later, continued to preach Christianity to the people in Northumbria.

11 Northumbria's Golden Age

A page from the Lindisfarne Gospels, written about AD 700. The first word, liber, *is the Latin name for 'book'*

1 Copy or trace the page from the Lindisfarne Gospels. Use colours to make it as beautiful as you can.
2 Can you make out the name which has been squeezed in by the writer at the end of the page?
3 Write down the capital letter of your first name and draw a pattern round it, as the monks did.

The Lindisfarne Gospels

During the late seventh and early eighth centuries, Northumbria became famous throughout Europe as a centre of learning and artistic skill. Monks in Northumbria produced many books for use in monastery schools in England and abroad. The finest of these is the Lindisfarne Gospels, made in the island monastery. Its pages, enriched with elaborate patterns, glow with a variety of bright colours. So much fine work was done that this period of time has been called the Golden Age of Northumbria.

King Oswy of Northumbria

The Celtic monks spread their message from the north of Britain and the missionaries of the Roman church from the south. This made difficulties because the two churches were different in many ways. For example, the two churches did not keep Easter at the same time. King Oswy belonged to the Celtic church but his wife had been baptized by Paulinus of the Roman church. So while the king was celebrating Easter his queen was still fasting for Lent. The king decided to hold a meeting to decide about the dating of Easter.

King Oswy makes up his mind

King Oswy smilingly asked them all: 'Tell me which is greater in the kingdom of heaven, Columba or the Apostle Peter?' The whole meeting answered with one voice: 'The Lord said this when he declared: "Thou art Peter and upon this rock I will build my church . . . . And I will give thee the keys to the kingdom of heaven . . . ." ' The king wisely replied: 'He is the porter and keeps the keys. With him I will have no differences.'

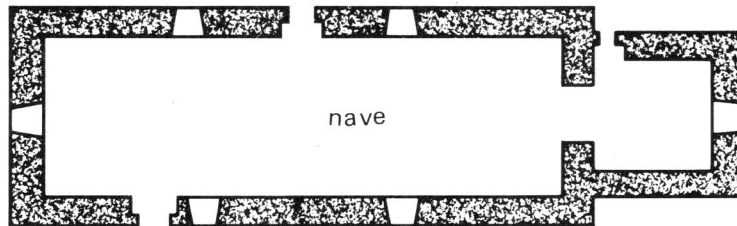

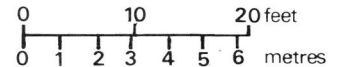

Taken from Eddius's Life of Wilfrid, *ch. 10, written in the seventh century*

nave

Escomb church, Co. Durham, was built in the late seventh century and is still standing today

4   Explain why King Oswy decided to follow the ways of the Roman church.
5   Work out the overall length and width of the nave of Escomb church.
6   Use the ground plan and the photograph to find out in what ways Escomb church has been changed since it was first built.
7   Why do you think Escomb church has survived to the present day?
8   Explain why the decision of King Oswy at the meeting at Whitby was important.

The meeting at Whitby

In AD 663 a meeting was called at the monastery at Whitby in Northumbria. The most important churchmen were present. Abbot Colman of Lindisfarne spoke first, saying that the Celtic church followed the customs of St Columba (see Opening 8) and other saints who had worked many miracles. Bishop Wilfrid of the Roman church replied by saying that Christians all over the rest of the world followed the rules of the Roman church. Finally King Oswy decided in favour of the Roman church. After this meeting at Whitby it was the Roman church, rather than the Celtic, which was the main church in England.

Escomb church

Most churches in Northumbria and the rest of Britain were made of wood at this time. However, a few stone churches, like St John's Church at Escomb near Durham, were built. It is one of the earliest stone churches still standing. Many of the stones used in making the walls of the church were taken from buildings dating from Roman times. Escomb church not only shows the fine workmanship but also the important place people gave to religion during the 'Golden Age of Northumbria'.

12 Bede the scholar

1 What is the monk holding in his right hand?
2 What might the sharp tool in his left hand be used for?
3 What creatures can you find in the decorated capital letter opposite?
4 Imagine what it was like to spend your days copying out books by hand. Explain the difficulties as well as the rewards of the task.

Bede's life

When Bede was seven, about AD 680, he entered a monastery in Northumbria. Two years later he moved to a new monastery nearby at Jarrow where he spent the rest of his life. Bede became a famous teacher and scholar. He wrote thirty-six books. On the last day of his life, although he was ill in bed, he continued the translation of a gospel from Latin into Anglo-Saxon. Bede told a monk to write his words down quickly because his 'heavenly birthday' was near. It was reported that just before he died Bede said, 'It is well finished. Glory be to the Father.'

Copying books

Scholars like Bede had every opportunity to study in monasteries which had collections of important books. Most monks spent a great deal of time copying out precious books by hand. They used quill pens which were usually large goose, swan or crow feathers sharpened to a fine point. They wrote on skin from sheep and goats which was called parchment. Monks took great pride in making ornamental pictures around capital letters. However, copying books for long periods of time could be hard and tedious work.

Angels not Angles

I must tell a story handed down to us which explains Pope Gregory's deep desire to see that the English people knew about God. We are told that one day when Gregory was passing through the market-place in Rome, he saw some boys being sold as slaves. Unlike the Roman people, these boys had pale complexions and fair hair. Gregory looked at the boys with interest and asked from what part of the world they came. 'From the island of Britain,' he was told, 'where all the people look like this.' Gregory then asked if these people were Christians. 'They do not believe in God — they are pagans,' he was told. 'Alas,' said Gregory with a sigh, 'how sad that such bright-faced folk do not know God! What is the name of these people?' 'They are Angles,' he was told. He replied, 'They have angelic faces — they should be called Angels, not Angles.' Later, when Gregory became Pope, he sent missionaries to the Angles and Saxons and prayed that their mission might be successful.

A famous story from Bede's History of the English Church and People, *Book 2, ch. 1*

5 Tell the story of Gregory and the boys in the market-place in Rome from the point of view of one of the boys.
6 What kind of man does the story show Pope Gregory to have been?
7 Why has Bede been called the 'father of English history'? Use the text below to give as many reasons as you can.
8 If you can find a feather perhaps you could try to write with it.

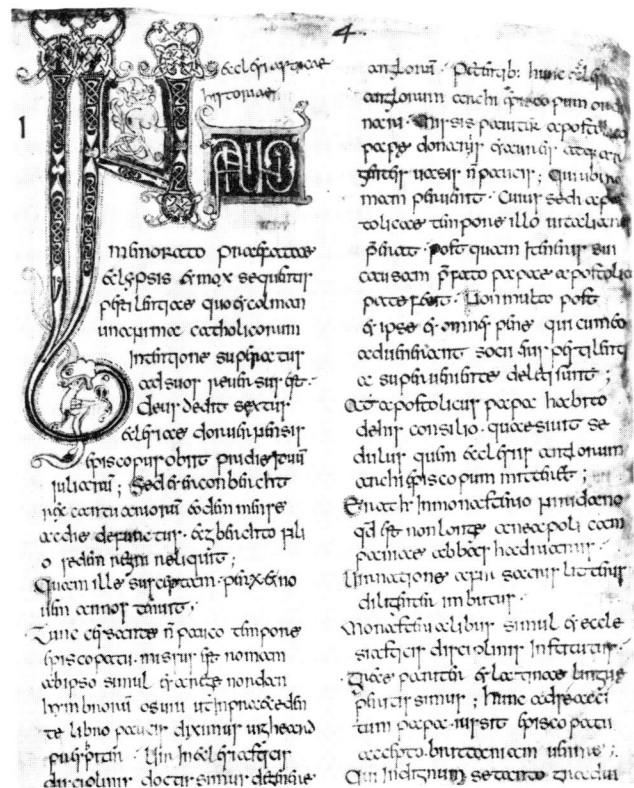

A page from Bede's History of the English Church and People, *copied by a monk about fifty years after Bede's death*

Bede's work

Bede's most famous book — *The History of the English Church and People* — was completed in AD 731. Bede wanted to find out all he could about the history of the Angles and Saxons. No one had done this before. He sent to many people all over the country asking for information. He tried hard to make sure that what he wrote was accurate and fair to people. His book tells most of what is known about the Anglo-Saxons or English people. After AD 735, when he died, many copies were made of his book. Bede is often called the 'father of English history'.

13 Law and order

Some of the laws of King Ine of Wessex (AD 688-94)

If anyone fights in the King's house, he is to lose all his possessions, and it is up to the King whether or not he shall lose his life too.

If he fights in the house of a peasant, he is to pay 120 shillings as a fine and 6 shillings to the peasant.

If anyone steals without his wife and children knowing, he is to pay 60 shillings as a fine, but if he steals with the knowledge of his household they all go into slavery.

If anyone burns down a tree in the wood and is found out, he is to pay full fine; he is to pay 60 shillings, for fire is a thief.

If a husband and wife have a child together and the husband dies, the mother is to keep her child and bring it up. She is to be given 6 shillings for its maintenance, a cow in summer, an ox in winter; the kinsmen are to look after the dead man's home until the child is grown up.

A woman appealing to a Saxon king for justice

1 Make a list of the crimes mentioned in Ine's laws.
2 Give examples from Ine's laws of how upholding the law and supporting the needy were the responsibility of everyone in the village.
3 Use the picture and Ine's laws to explain the importance of the king with regard to the law.

The price of a man

It was the duty of Saxon kings to draw up laws. It was the responsibility of the people to see that the laws were not broken. As there was no police force they were expected to catch offenders in their village and bring them before the court, or 'moot'. The basic idea of Saxon law was that a person who did wrong to someone else should pay him compensation. The amount of money to be paid depended on a person's worth. Every man had his own price, or 'wergild'. If a man was killed, his price had to be paid to his family.

Oaths

Our modern laws have developed largely from Roman and Saxon laws. However, different methods from those of today were used for proving guilt. If a man were accused of a crime he could either admit or deny it. If he admitted guilt, he paid the fine due. If he denied it, he had to prove that he was innocent by swearing an oath that he had not committed the crime. He tried to gather a number of friends from the village who would swear to his innocence. They were called oath-helpers, and if he found enough to support him he was set free.

Murder in the village

One night Edwin, lord of a village in Wessex, was found dead with a sword through his stomach. A servant claimed that when he had last seen his lord he was drinking with one of his warriors, Uffa, and that the two men had been arguing loudly. Uffa was brought to the village moot and swore that he had not committed the murder. However he was a man of such bad character, that no one would swear to his innocence. There was only one course of action left: he must be tried by ordeal — the judgment of God. He was taken to the church where he was made to pick up a red-hot iron bar and to carry it for nine feet. His hands were then bandaged and three days later the priest removed the bandages. Festering sores covered Uffa's fingers: the wounds had not healed cleanly — he was guilty! So serious was his crime of killing his lord, that no fine was sufficient to compensate. He was hanged.

This story was written by a modern author to show how Saxon law worked

A hanged man, from a Saxon manuscript

A person's worth in the kingdom of Wessex, before the time of King Alfred

King's warrior	1200 shillings
Lord of the village	600 shillings
Freeman	200 shillings
Slave	nothing

4   Re-tell the story above from the point of view of either Edwin's wife or Uffa.
5   Explain why trials by ordeal were thought by Saxons to be the judgment of God.
6   How fair do you think Saxon methods of proving a person innocent or guilty were?
7   How do our methods of trial today differ from those of the Saxons?

Ordeal and punishment

If the accused could not prove his innocence by oath, he was tried by ordeal. In one trial he was tied up and thrown into a pond. If he floated, he was guilty. In another he had to put his arm up to the elbow in boiling water to lift out a stone. If the arm healed cleanly, he was innocent. A guilty man was punished. A fine was the usual penalty, but if the offender could not pay, or if the crime was very serious, there were harsher punishments. For example, thieves might have a hand or a foot cut off.

The ordeal of the red-hot bar (an artist's impression)

14 Saxon kings and kingdoms

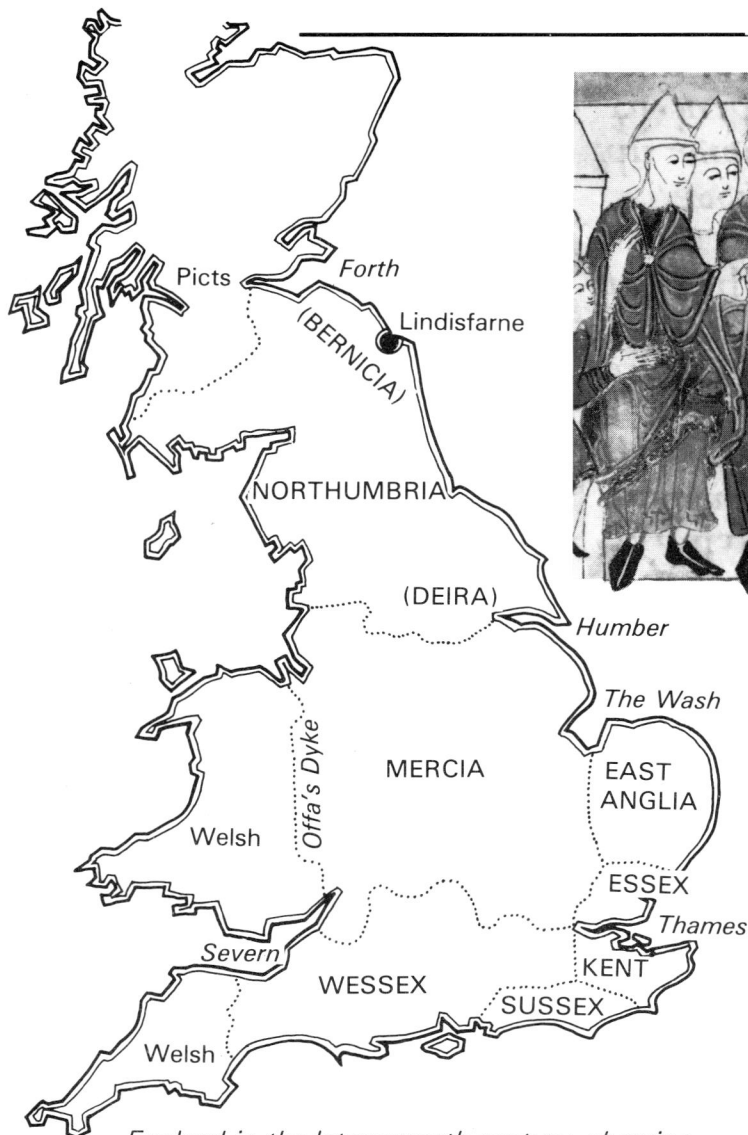

England in the later seventh century, showing the seven kingdoms

A Saxon king and his council

1 List the seven English kingdoms in the seventh century.
2 Which two kingdoms covered the largest area of land?
3 How can you tell who is the king in the picture? How many members are there in his council?
4 Use the text below to make a list of the main duties of a king's council. Explain why each of its duties was very important.

Saxon kings

The Saxons chose kings for their skill as leaders and warriors in war. In early times it was believed that kings were descended from the gods. They were responsible for making laws (see Opening 13) and protecting the people. In return subjects were expected to be loyal to the king. By the seventh century England was divided into seven kingdoms. Some were not much larger than today's counties, while others covered large areas of England. Our words king and kingdom come from the Saxon 'cyning' and 'cynedom'.

The Witan

Saxon kings in England were usually assisted by a council of wise men called a Witengemot. (Witena — wise, gemot — council). It was often called Witan for short. The Witan was composed of experienced people from the king's family and his warriors. When kings became Christian, churchmen joined the Witan. The Witan met at Christmas, Easter and Whitsuntide and at times of emergency. Its main duties were to choose the most suitable king when the previous one died, and to advise the king on peace and war and making laws.

(the kings who ruled over both kingdoms are in capital letters)

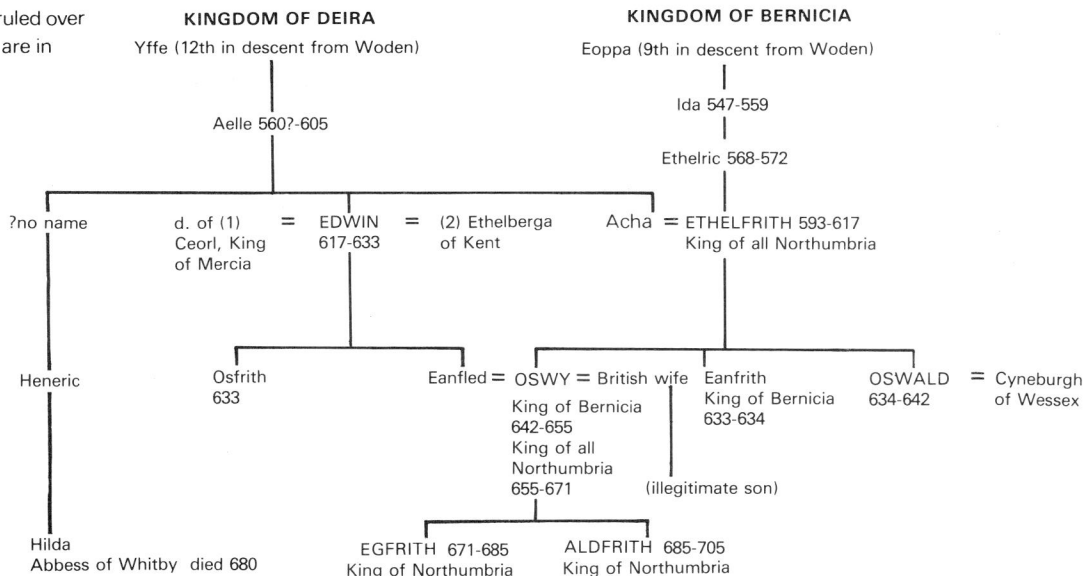

KINGDOM OF DEIRA
Yffe (12th in descent from Woden)

KINGDOM OF BERNICIA
Eoppa (9th in descent from Woden)

Ida 547-559

Ethelric 568-572

Aelle 560?-605

?no name

d. of (1) Ceorl, King of Mercia = EDWIN 617-633 = (2) Ethelberga of Kent

Acha = ETHELFRITH 593-617 King of all Northumbria

Heneric

Osfrith 633

Eanfled = OSWY King of Bernicia 642-655 King of all Northumbria 655-671 = British wife

Eanfrith King of Bernicia 633-634

OSWALD 634-642 = Cyneburgh of Wessex

(illegitimate son)

Hilda Abbess of Whitby died 680

EGFRITH 671-685 King of Northumbria

ALDFRITH 685-705 King of Northumbria

Northumbrian kings — a family tree

5 Use the Northumbrian family tree to name the following: (a) the two areas which were united to form the kingdom of Northumbria; (b) the god from whom the early kings believed they were descended; (c) The Christian queen of Edwin; (d) the first king of all Northumbria; (e) the marriage which marked the uniting of the two Northumbrian royal families; (f) the king who was father of two kings of Northumbria; (g) the English kingdoms that provided queens for Northumbrian kings; (h) the lady from the royal family of Deira who became a famous abbess.

6 Imagine you are a member of a Witan of a kingdom that is being invaded by enemies and where the law is often being broken. Make a list of the qualities you would like the man whom you elect king to have.

7 Use the text below to draw a diagram with pictures to show the achievements of King Offa of Mercia.

A silver penny of King Offa of Mercia

The kingdom of Northumbria
During the seventh century Northumbria became the most important of the seven kingdoms in England. The main reason for this was the powerful kings. Between them they defeated their enemies — the Picts in the north and the kings of Mercia — and united their people. A turning point came when King Edwin became a Christian (see Opening 10). Following this, Northumbrian kings encouraged Christian preaching and learning with people like St Aidan, St Cuthbert (see Opening 9) and St Hilda.

King Offa of Mercia
Mercia became the most powerful kingdom in the eighth century. Offa (757-96) was Mercia's greatest king. He made an alliance with Northumbria, whose king married Offa's daughter. He defeated the king of East Anglia. He made two expeditions against the Welsh and built a dyke to mark his western boundary. London became a Mercian city. Offa minted silver pennies which were used throughout the country and trade was developed with the continent. He also set up a strong code of laws. Offa was acknowledged king of the English, but Mercia's power did not last. The Vikings were about to attack.

15 Saxon Britain, AD 400-800

EVENTS

*c.*410 Withdrawal of Roman legions from Britain

King Arthur defeats Saxons

563 St Columba went to Iona

*c.*588 Gregory saw Anglo-Saxon slaves in Ron

Invasions of Angles and Saxons

463 Death of St Patrick

King Arthur defeated Saxons at Battle of Bladon(?)

597 St Augustine converted Kir Ethelbert

400   450   500   550

RELIGION

Mission of St Patrick to Ireland **432-61**

St Patrick

Work of St Columb **563-97**

Pope Gregory 1 **590-604**

KINGS

Ethelbert, king of Kent *c.***560-616**

1   Make a list of the men and women who became saints.
2   List the kings who helped the development of Christianity.
3   The time chart begins and ends with invasions of England. Name these invaders.
4   Which king on the time chart reigned longest?

St Augustine

1 St Augustine became Archbishop of Canterbury

5 King Ethelfrith united Northumbria

7 King Edwin of Northumbria baptized by St Paulinus

25-55 Sutton Hoo ship burial

1 King Oswald slain in battle with Penda of Mercia

Bede

663 Synod of Whitby

687 Death of St Cuthbert

c. **700-50** Poem 'Beowulf' was written

731 Bede's 'History of the English Church and People' completed

774 King Offa was called 'King of the English'

793 Vikings raid Lindisfarne

650   700   750   800

Aidan's mission in Northumbria **634-51**

Work of St Cuthbert **650-87**

St Hilda, Abbess of Whitby **657-80**

Theodore, Archbishop of Canterbury **669-90**

Lindisfarne Gospels *c.* **700-20**

win, king of Northumbria **617-33**

wald, king of Northumbria **634-41**

wy, king of Northumbria **641-70**

Ine, king of Wessex **688-94**

Ethelbald, king of Mercia **716-57**

Offa, king of Mercia **757-96**

Edwin of Northumbria

5 Use the time chart to write an account of the religious developments in Northumbria between 617 and 687.

6 What new information have you discovered from the time chart?

7 The Saxons made a considerable contribution to the development of Britain. Write a brief account of their achievements under the headings: kings and kingdoms, law, Christianity, place-names.

16 Viking invaders

A tombstone from Lindisfarne monastery, which many archaeologists think shows a Viking attack. It was carved in about AD 793

The attack on Lindisfarne

And they came to the church of Lindisfarne, laid everything waste with terrible plundering, trampled the holy places with polluted feet, dug up the altars and seized all the treasures of the holy church. They killed some of the brothers, took some away with them in chains, many they drove out naked and insulted, some they drowned in the sea.

from History of the Kings *written by a monk, Symeon of Durham, about AD 1100*

1 What weapons are being carried by the warriors?
2 For what kind of person do you think this tombstone was made?
3 Why do you think the Vikings came to Britain?
4 Imagine that you arrived at Lindisfarne just after the Vikings had left. Write a description of what you might have found there.

The Vikings attack

By AD 790 about 350 years had passed since the Saxons invaded Britain. Most had settled as farmers and believed in the Christian faith. It was a great shock when fierce Viking warriors suddenly began to invade the country. In AD 793 a Viking raiding party attacked the monastery at Lindisfarne. Later Jarrow monastery, where Bede had lived, and the monastery on Iona were plundered. People in every village on the coasts of Britain feared attacks from these pagan raiders from the sea. The monk Alcuin of York wrote at this time, 'never before has such a terror appeared in Britain'!

On their raids the Vikings were looking mainly for treasure, which they found in the rich monasteries. They killed and burned, and it is not surprising that a new verse was added to church prayers: 'From the fury of the Northmen, good Lord deliver us.' Vikings came from the lands which today are called Norway, Sweden and Denmark. At first the Vikings sailed to Britain in summer and seized what treasure they could before returning home before the winter storms. Later, because there was a shortage of farming land in their homelands, many Vikings decided to settle in Britain.

King Edmund of East Anglia and Vikings

The year 870
In this year the Viking host went across Mercia into East Anglia and took winter-quarters at Thetford; and in the same winter St Edmund the King fought against them and the Vikings won the victory, and they slew the king and overran the entire kingdom and destroyed all the monasteries to which they came. At that same time they came to the monastery at Medeshsmatede [Peterborough] and burned and demolished it, and slew the abbot and monks and all that they found there, reducing to nothing what had once been a very rich monastery.

from the Anglo-Saxon Chronicle

5   Imagine you are a monk behind the King Edmund's throne and describe what is happening to the king.
6   Why did the Saxon monks dislike the Vikings so much?
7   Why are the only written records about the Viking invasions written by monks?
8   From books find out all you can about the death of King Edmund of East Anglia. What town in East Anglia is named after him?

The Vikings in England

From about AD 835 hardly a year went by without a Viking raid being reported in the *Anglo-Saxon Chronicle* — a diary written by monks with an entry for every year instead of every day. In AD 851 the *Chronicle* recorded: 'In this year . . . for the first time, heathen men stayed through the winter in Thanet. And in the same year three hundred ships came into the mouth of the Thames and stormed Canterbury and London.' The Vikings carried out fierce and frequent attacks. In AD 866 the *Chronicle* reported a 'great army' which, starting out from East Anglia, began to march through the land, looting and destroying.

First the Viking army marched north and stormed York. Next it invaded Mercia, where only the payment of money persuaded the warriors to leave. Then the army returned to East Anglia, robbing as it went and, according to legend, killing King Edmund. By AD 871 the Vikings had won victories in the north and midlands and were preparing to invade the remaining Saxon kingdom, Wessex (see Openings 17 and 18). The Vikings have been described as fierce and warlike. But we must remember that the only written records of their invasion were by monks who had every reason to fear them.

17 Alfred the Great 1

King Alfred's family

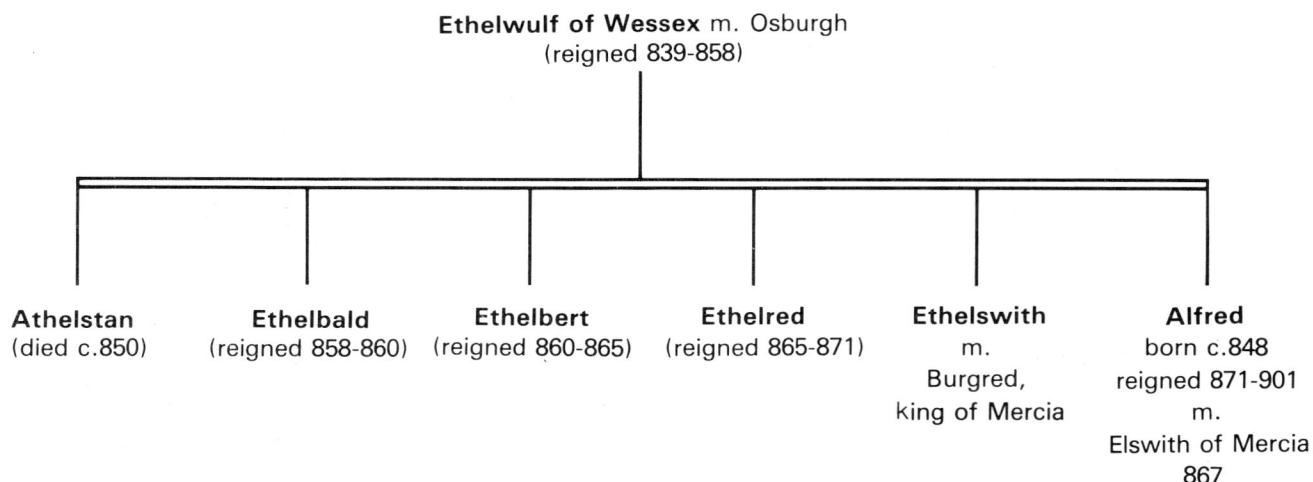

Ethelwulf of Wessex m. Osburgh
(reigned 839-858)

Athelstan (died c.850)	**Ethelbald** (reigned 858-860)	**Ethelbert** (reigned 860-865)	**Ethelred** (reigned 865-871)	**Ethelswith** m. Burgred, king of Mercia	**Alfred** born c.848 reigned 871-901 m. Elswith of Mercia 867

1   What was the name of Alfred's mother and father?
2   How many brothers did Alfred have?
3   Which brother never became a king?
4   What do you notice about the length of time each of Alfred's brothers ruled?
5   Why, when Alfred was born, was it not expected that he would ever be king?
6   How old was Alfred when he became king?
7   Tell the story of Alfred and the book as his mother might have told it (see below).

A silver penny of King Alfred

Alfred's early life

No other king in English history had been called 'Great'. However it was not expected that Alfred would ever be king although he was born a son of the king of Wessex. Before he was seven, he had made two visits to Rome to meet the Pope. He became a devoted Christian. Alfred, as a boy, was also interested in books and learning as well as hunting. However the invasions of the Vikings meant that he had to learn how to fight at an early age. He helped his father and his brothers defend the kingdom of Wessex against Viking attacks.

Alfred and the book

One famous story of the young Alfred was told by the monk Asser who came to Alfred's court about AD 884. He became one of the king's closest advisers. 'One day Alfred's mother showed a book of Saxon poetry to Alfred and his brothers and said, "I will give this book to whoever learns it first." Inspired by these words . . . Alfred took the book to his teacher. When Alfred knew it by heart he went back to his mother and repeated it. Alfred won the book' (Asser's *Life of King Alfred*, written about AD 893).

The *Anglo-Saxon Chronicle* gives a year-by-year account of Alfred's fight against the Vikings

AD 878. In this year in mid-winter the enemy army came stealthily to Chippenham. It occupied the land of the West Saxons and settled there . . . and the people submitted to them, except King Alfred. At Easter King Alfred made a stronghold with a small force at Athelney. Then after Easter he rode (eastwards) and all the people . . . rejoiced to see him. He went to Edington and there fought against the whole army and put it to flight. Then the enemy gave hostages and swore great oaths that they would leave his kingdom. They also promised that their king, Guthrum, would be baptized.

8 Why was King Alfred's statue at Winchester erected in 1901? The family tree opposite will help you.
9 Can we know what King Alfred looked like? How far do the coin and the statue help us?
10 How reliable do you think the two stories about King Alfred are (below)? Give reasons for your answer.
11 Draw a diagram or chart to show the various ways in which King Alfred defeated the Vikings.

Statue of Alfred at Winchester

King Alfred the warrior
Two stories from the twelfth century about Alfred:
1 'Alfred hid in the home of a cowherd. The cowherd's wife was cooking some loaves. The king was sitting by the fire sharpening weapons. Presently the woman saw the loaves burning. "Why can't you turn them when you see them burning?" she cried. The woman had no idea that he was King Alfred.'
2 'Alfred entered the tent of the Viking king disguised as a minstrel. He went into the banqueting room and wasted no opportunity of learning the king's secrets both with eyes and ears.'

Alfred was determined to drive the Vikings out of Wessex. He fought them throughout his reign on land and at sea. Alfred was an energetic and skilful leader. He wanted a well-trained army. He gave orders that all fit men in Wessex should do six months' service in the army each year while the remainder continued work on their farms. Then the two groups exchanged places. He also formed a royal bodyguard of brave warriors. He established forts — called burghs — for defence against the invasions of the Vikings. Alfred realized he must defeat the enemy before they landed. He had a fleet of ships built. He is often called the founder of the English navy.

18 Alfred the Great 2

Statue of King Alfred at Wantage, where he was born

1 What is King Alfred shown holding in his hands in the statue at Wantage?
2 In what ways does this statue give a different view of Alfred compared with the Winchester statue (Opening 17)?
3 Describe the portrait on Alfred's jewel.
4 No one is sure what the jewel was used for. What do you think might have been its use? Give reasons for your answer.

Alfred's jewel, made by Saxon craftsmen. It is 6.4 centimetres long and 2.6 centimetres wide

King Alfred and learning

Alfred did not spend all his time fighting the Vikings. He wanted to encourage learning in England. He gathered scholars at his court from Britain and abroad. For example, Asser came from Wales. It was Asser who taught the king to read Latin when Alfred was about forty years old, and helped in the translation of the religious books so that more people could read them. Alfred also set up schools where sons of his nobles were taught to read and write. King Alfred was also interested in history and it was probably he who encouraged monks to write the *Anglo-Saxon Chronicle*.

King Alfred's craftsmen

The jewel shown above dates from the time of King Alfred. It is made of gold and has an enamelled portrait. The base of the jewel is hollow and is shaped like an animal's head. Around the edge the inscription reads: 'Aelfred mec heht gewyrcan' — 'Alfred had me made.' The jewel was found near Athelney in Somerset. Asser tells us that Alfred set aside one-sixth of the money of the kingdom to pay craftsmen to make beautiful objects like bells, crosses and candlesticks for churches. Unfortunately only a few of these have survived.

The king was wounded by the nails of many troubles. From his twentieth to his forty-fifth year (in which he now is) he has been troubled by a . . . severe unknown disease. He was troubled too by the constant attacks of foreign peoples by land and sea. What shall I say of his many battles against the heathen, of the ceaseless problems of being king? What of the cities and towers he has restored and the new ones he has built . . . ? What of the royal halls and chambers built of stone and wood at his command? He stood alone, dependent on help from God, like a skilful helmsman struggling to bring his ship to a safe harbour . . . .

from Asser's Life of King Alfred *(see Opening 17)*

5 What does the picture on the right tell you about Saxon kings?
6 What new information about King Alfred does the extract from Asser give?
7 Was Asser likely to be critical of, or sympathetic to, Alfred?
8 Saxons liked ballads (poems which told a story). Write a ballad about the achievements of Alfred the Great.

A detailed picture of a king, from a Saxon manuscript

King Alfred and the church

King Alfred had new stone churches built, and monasteries were set up at Athelney and Winchester. Alfred encouraged monks and priests to teach the people. They also helped him to rule his kingdom. Churchmen were ready to support the king because, after the Vikings had settled, few Christian kings were left in Britain. Moreover King Alfred kept law and order justly. He gathered together all the previous laws and chose the best ones. Before his death King Alfred wrote, 'I desired to live worthily and leave to the men who should come after, my memory in good works.'

The inscription on King Alfred's statue at Wantage set up in 1877 reads:

Alfred Found Learning Dead,
And He restored It.
Education Neglected
And he Revived It,
The Laws Powerless
And He Gave Them Force,
The Church Debased
And He Raised It,
The Land Ravaged
By a Fearful Enemy
From Which He Delivered It.

19 Viking place-names

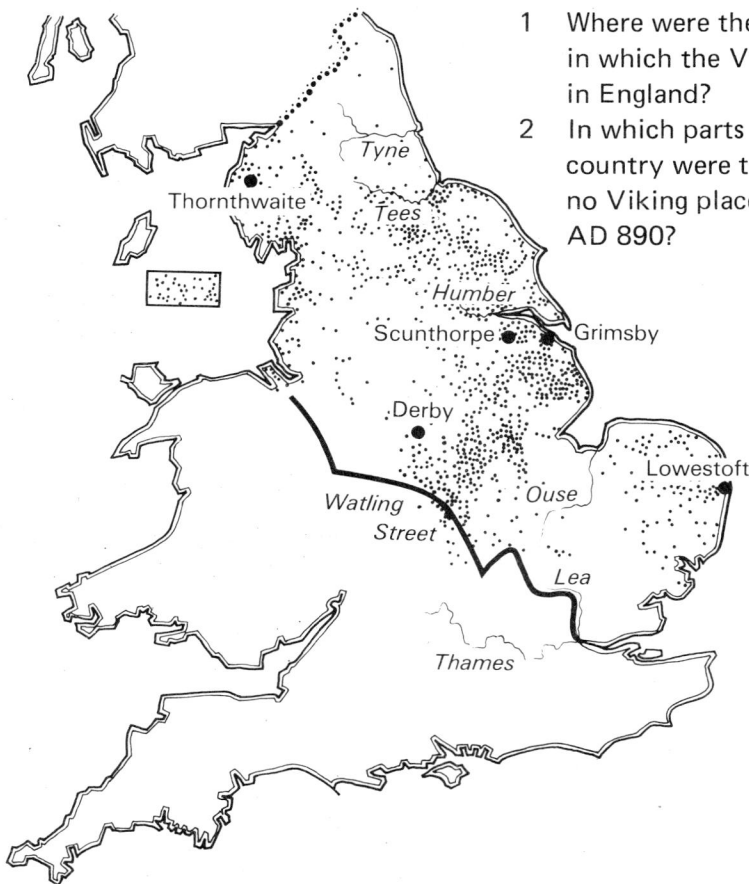

Map of Viking settlements

The axe was the favourite weapon of the Vikings in both war and peace. It was used to clear the forests in order to make clearings for home-steads

1. Where were the main areas in which the Vikings settled in England?
2. In which parts of the country were there few or no Viking place-names by AD 890?
3. Use the text below to explain the meaning of the following Viking place-names: Applethwaite, Frankby and Grassthorpe.
4. Use the text below to work out the Viking place-names for the following: the river crossing named after Knut; a clearing in a wood where long thin sticks (staves) were cut; a clearing in a forest near a hollow (dingle).

Viking place-names

Viking settlements can be traced through place-names. The most common Viking place-name endings are:

- BY — a village
- LEIGH, LEE or LEY — a clearing in a forest
- THORPE — a village or hamlet
- THWAITE — a meadow or clearing
- TOFT — a farmstead

The Vikings made up their place-names in much the same way as the Saxons. They were often named after a chief:

- Grim and his people called their village GRIMSBY.
- Kettil and his people called their hamlet KETTLETHORPE.

Places were often named after features of the landscape:

- There were many deer near one village so it was called Deer-by — DERBY.

The Danelaw

Eastern England which was given to the Vikings by the agreement of AD 886 was called the Danelaw. Sometimes the Vikings renamed the

The treaty between King Alfred and King Guthrum AD 886

This is the peace which King Alfred and King Guthrum and the Councillors of all the English and all the people in East Anglia have agreed on and confirmed with oaths, binding themselves and their subjects, for the living and the unborn.

1 First concerning our boundaries [between the Saxons to the West and the Vikings to the East], up the Thames and then up the [river] Lee, and along the Lee to its source and then in a straight line to Bedford then up the [river] Ouse to Watling Street [an old Roman road].

5 How does the agreement between Alfred and Guthrum explain the whereabouts of Viking settlements in England?

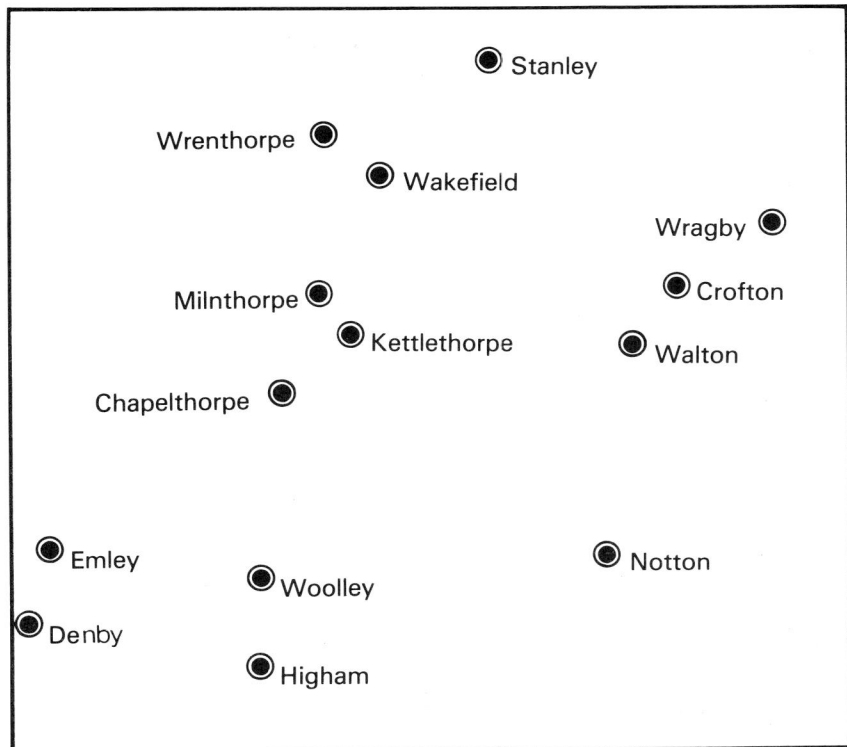

Place-names in the area of Wakefield, Yorkshire

◉ Stanley

Wrenthorpe ◉

◉ Wakefield

Wragby ◉

◉ Crofton

Milnthorpe ◉

◉ Kettlethorpe

◉ Walton

Chapelthorpe ◉

◉ Emley

◉ Notton

◉ Woolley

◉ Denby

◉ Higham

6 Make a list of place-names under three headings: *Anglo-Saxon place-names, Viking place-names* and *Either Saxon or Viking place-names* of places in the Wakefield area of Yorkshire (see also Opening 7).

7 Use a map of the Lake District (Cumbria) to make a list of some of the places with Viking names.

8 Use a map to study the place-names of the area in which you live, and make a list of any Viking names.

Saxon villages which they had taken over. They also settled in many new villages. Few written records or graves have survived from the Danelaw so the evidence provided by place-names is very important. We know from the Domesday Book — a register of land and possessions made by King William the Conqueror in 1086 — that there were 800 Viking place-names ending in 'by' south of the River Tees, while in Yorkshire alone over 30 per cent of the place-names were Viking.

The Lake District

The Lake District is an interesting area for studying Viking place-names. Between AD 900 and 950 Vikings from the land which today is called Norway crossed the North Sea and settled in the north-west of England. For this reason many of the place-names in this area are made up of endings like — thwaite and —wick (creek or bay). Many natural features have Viking names, for example: beck (stream), fell (hill or mountain), force (waterfall), gill (a deep valley with a stream), keld (a well or spring of water), scar (cliff) and tarn (a small lake).

20 Viking longships

A replica of a Viking longship which was sailed across the Atlantic in 1893

1 Describe the replica of a Viking longship.
2 Design an animal prow for a Viking longship.
3 Why do you think people wanted to build and to sail a modern reconstruction of a Viking longship?
4 Imagine you were the man standing before the mast in the leading ship in *Njal's Saga* (below). Describe how you would have felt.

Descriptions of the longships

A fleet of Viking longships was a splendid sight. A description of the fleet which Canute (Opening 27) brought to England in 1015 reads: 'So great was the decoration of the ships that the eyes of those who saw them were dazzled, and to those looking from a distance, they seemed to be of flame rather than of wood . . . . The flashing of armour shone in one place, and in another the flame of suspended shields. Gold shone on the prows . . . . So great, in fact, was the magnificence of the fleet . . . that the ships alone would have terrified the English people.'

A Viking story called *Njal's Saga* contains another vivid description of a fleet approaching to attack: 'Some ships came sweeping round the head-land, making straight for the enemy. War shields lined the sides and before the mast of the leading vessel stood a man who wore a gilded helmet and carried a spear.' However, for those on board ship life could be hard. The only cover against rain and sea was a sheet drawn over the centre of the ship, and water had to be baled out in rough weather. Men slept crowded together on the floor in skin sleeping bags.

5 Draw the Gokstad ship and label the following: keel, planks, holes for oars, stump of the mast.

6 Imagine you were an archaeologist who had just found the carved stone. What could you learn about Viking ships from it and what questions would you ask about what is shown on the stone?

A Viking ship, carved in the eighth century on a stone in Sweden

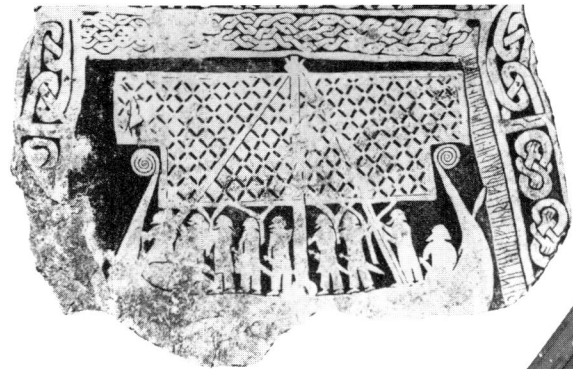

7 The Vikings gave their ships exciting names. Think of some of your own and write them down.

8 How do you think the Vikings navigated their ships?

A reconstructed Viking ship, 24 metres long, found in a burial mound at Gokstad in Sweden, and dating from about AD 900

The speed of the longships

A good deal is known about the ships in which the Vikings came to Britain. This is because well-preserved examples have been excavated from burial mounds in Norway. The reason why the Vikings could make long and dangerous sea voyages was that they had learned to build strong, swift ships. They were longer and deeper than Saxon ships. The sides were made of overlapping oak panels fastened to a framework. A large wooden paddle for steering was fixed to the right hand side of the vessel, the 'steerboard' side — from which comes the word 'starboard'.

Vikings loved the speed of ships and so gave them names such as 'Wave Walker', 'Raven of the Wind' and 'Dark Horse of the Sea'. Although oars were used in calm weather, ships were usually propelled by means of a great square sail. This was often striped or chequered in red, blue, green and white, and was controlled by a system of ropes fastened along the lower edge. A weather-vane was used to find out the direction of the wind. The carved head of a savage animal, covered in gold and silver, usually decorated both prow and stern.

21 Viking gods and graves

A carved stone dating from the eighth century, found in Gotland, Sweden

1 *Battle scene with birds of prey*
2 *A dead warrior is carried from the battle by Odin's eight-legged horse*
3 *The warrior's spirit rides to Valhalla*

Stone statue of Odin   *Bronze statue of Thor*

1 Describe what you can see in the first scene on the Gotland stone.
2 Use the Gotland stone to write an account of what happened to the warrior from the time he was killed in battle to his entry into Valhalla.
3 How do you think the archaeologists who found the statues knew they were of the gods Odin and Thor?
4 In what way did the Vikings believe that it was best for a man to die?

Heaven and hell

The Vikings who settled in Britain were not Christians. They believed in many gods who, they thought, lived in a great walled city. Within the city was an enormous hall called Valhalla, which was heaven. The spirits of warriors killed in battle went to Valhalla, where they would enjoy feasting and fighting until the end of the world should come. A rainbow bridge linked heaven and earth. Round the earth was a deep ocean filled with monsters. Beneath the earth was the sad, misty land to which passed the spirits of all who did not die in battle.

The gods

The Vikings believed that the three most important gods were Odin, Thor and Frey. One-eyed Odin, the greatest god, was wise and cunning, attended by twelve warrior maidens, the Valkyries, who brought the souls of those who died in battle to Valhalla. Red-bearded Thor was the most popular god. He carried a hammer which he used in his fight against the giants, the enemies of the gods. The handsome Frey was the god of love and farming. The Vikings believed that one day the gods and the whole world would be destroyed by monsters.

An artist's impression of a ship cremation

5 What evidence remains in the ground which tells an archaeologist that a ship cremation has taken place there?

6 Why do you think Vikings were usually buried surrounded by their possessions?

7 Imagine you were the son or wife of a Viking warrior who had died in battle. Describe the various ceremonies of the ship cremation.

8 List some of the main differences between the Christian and Viking religions.

Funerals

When Vikings died they were either buried or cremated. The dead person was dressed in his own clothing and jewellery and surrounded by food, weapons, tools and furniture. Sometimes dogs, horses and occasionally slaves were killed and their bodies laid nearby. Often the corpse was placed inside a wooden burial chamber. Everything was then buried in the earth or set on fire. Sometimes Vikings were buried in their longships. In AD 922 an Arab traveller saw the ship cremation of a Viking chieftain and described the ceremony.

'Then they brought ale, fruit and sweet-smelling plants and laid them by him; they also brought bread, meat and leeks and threw them in front of him . . . . Next they brought all his weapons and laid them beside him . . . . Then the people came forward with wood and timber; each brought a stick with its tip on fire and threw it on the wood lying under the ship, so that the flames took hold, first on the wood and then on the ship . . . and everything inside the ship. Thereupon a strong wind arose, so that the flames grew fiercer and the fire blazed.'

22 Viking warriors

1 Identify the pieces of equipment for battle in the picture.
2 Write down exciting names that a Viking warrior might have given to each.

Viking arms and armour from museums in Scandinavia

Battles

Weapons were most important to Viking men. They were laid beside the dead in their graves (Opening 21), and to the living they were prized possessions. To fight bravely in battle was the best way to win glory. The stories, or sagas, which Vikings handed down from one generation to the next tell of heroic exploits of great warriors. Battles usually consisted of combats between pairs or groups of men. Victories were won more by surprise and ferocity than by careful planning. Sometimes before battle, warriors would work themselves up into a savage frenzy yelling and biting their shields so that they would fight more boldly. During the first part of a battle, spears and arrows were thrown at the enemy from a distance. In the sagas, spears were called by names such as 'the flying dragon of the wounds' and 'the serpent of the battle'. Next the warriors closed in for hand-to-hand fighting, hacking and slashing with heavy swords and battle-axes. Swords were things of beauty, with hilts often inlaid with patterns of gold, silver and copper. They were passed down from father to son and many had their own names. King Magnus's sword was called 'Leg-biter'!

An ivory chess-piece showing a Viking warrior before battle

3 What is the Viking warrior (chess-piece) doing?
4 Draw a Viking warrior using some of the weapons and armour above.
5 Make a list of the weapons and describe the armour in the battle scene.
6 A Saxon king is shown in the picture. What happened to him?
7 Imagine you are a Viking poet or story-teller. Describe the exploits of a warrior in battle.

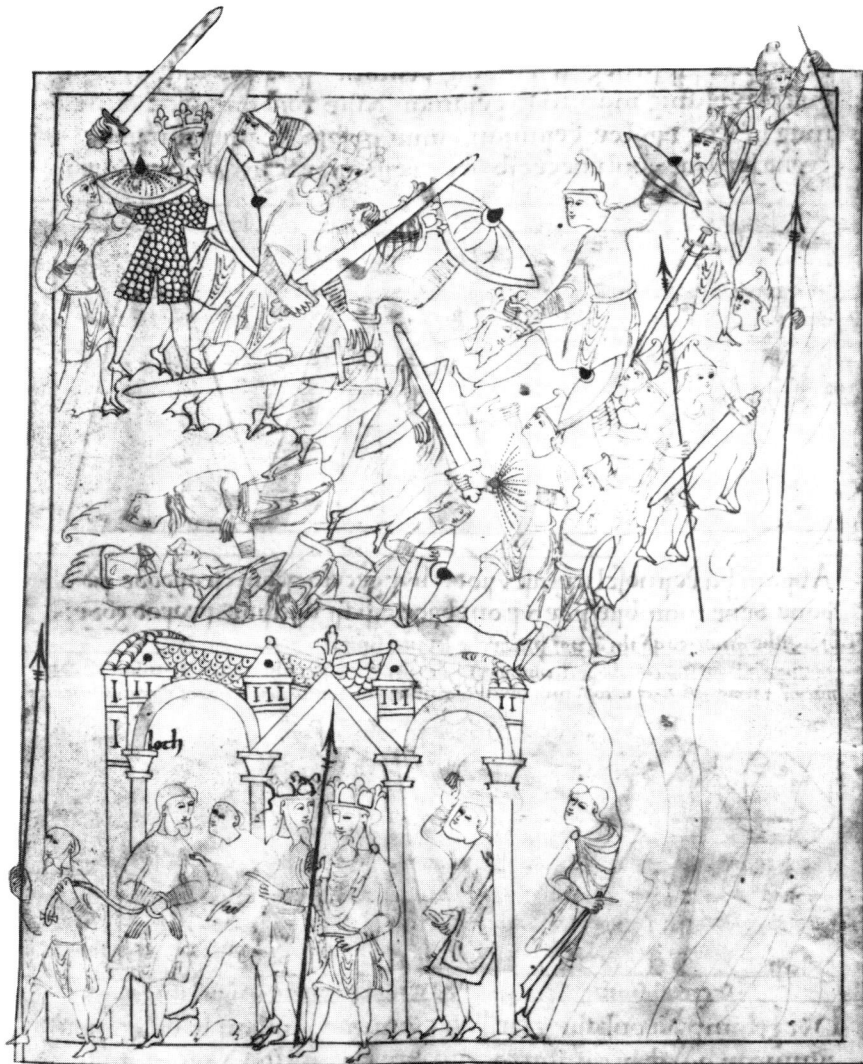

A battle between Saxon and Viking warriors

Battle-axes

These eventually became the favourite weapons. Their blades could measure as much as 30 centimetres across, and their 120 centimetre-long shafts needed two hands to wield them. These fearsome weapons could cut off an enemy's hands, feet or head. This description of the axe's power comes from *Njal's Saga*: 'Just as Thrain was putting on his helmet, Skarphedin swept up to him. He swung up his axe and crashed it down on Thrain's head splitting it down to the jaws . . . . ' Because defensive armour was light, warriors depended on agility and speed to dodge the blows aimed at them.

Armour

Most Vikings went into battle with a light shield as the only protection. Shields were made of wooden boards, bound together by iron bars with a round boss in the centre to protect the fingers. They were used to ward off blows or could be smashed into an enemy's face. Helmets were conical in shape and made of leather or metal and sometimes had nose and cheek pieces added. Wealthy chieftains had the additional protection of helmets which covered the whole head and face and of coats of mail made of interlocking rings.

23 Excavation at Viking York 1

A view of the excavation in Coppergate, York, in the summer of 1976

1 Describe the various types of work the archaeologists are doing in the picture.

2 What problems do you think faced the archaeologists as they excavated this site?

3 What are the main kinds of sources that provide us with evidence about Viking York?

Viking York

York, where St Paulinus had first preached Christianity in the north (see Opening 10), was the capital of the Saxon kingdom of Northumbria for over three centuries. However, in AD 867 it was captured by Viking invaders. For nearly sixty years afterwards York and the area between the rivers Humber and Tweed was ruled by Viking kings. In AD 927 King Athelstan, the first king to claim to rule over the whole of England (see Opening 25), marched north and defeated the Vikings. Later, in AD 954, the last Viking king of York, Eric Bloodaxe, was defeated and driven out of England.

The evidence for life in Viking York

English kings appointed earls to rule York after AD 954 but the Viking way of life remained strong. Information about Viking York can be found from various sources. For example a passage in the *Life of St Oswald*, written about AD 1000, says, '. . . not fewer than thirty thousand men and women are numbered in the city which is filled with the riches of merchants coming from everywhere, especially from the Danish [Viking] nation'. The evidence of place-names is useful. The modern name of the city comes from its Viking name — Jorvik. The Viking name for street was 'gate'. Over forty streets in York

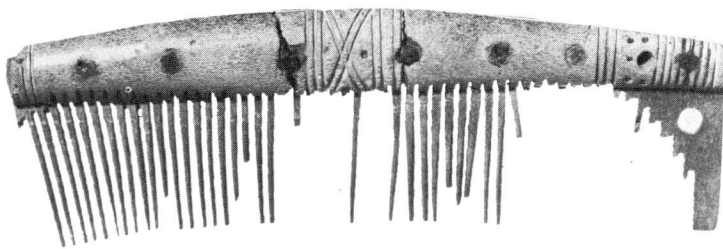

A bone comb, dating from about AD1000, found at Coppergate

A diagram showing how the skate was probably attached to the boot. One leather strap was pegged into a hole in the back of the skate and the other was wound round the toe

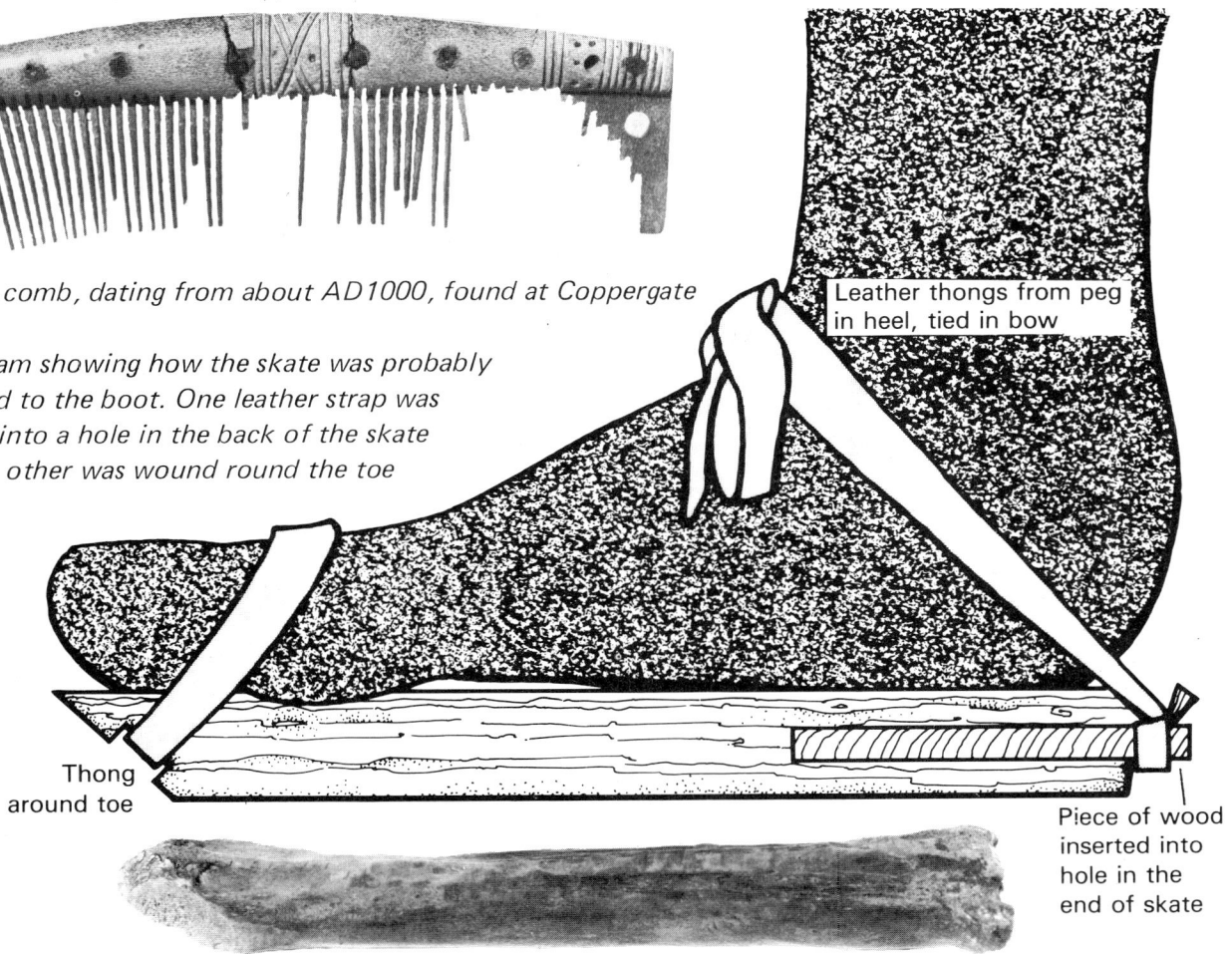

Leather thongs from peg in heel, tied in bow

Thong around toe

Piece of wood inserted into hole in the end of skate

A skate, made from the thighbone of an animal, which was found at Coppergate

4 Explain why many objects made from bone have survived. How old is the comb?

5 Describe in your own words how the bone was used as a skate.

have names ending in gate, for example Goodramgate and Coppergate.

The excavation at Coppergate

During the last one hundred years some evidence for life in Viking York has been provided by objects found by archaeologists. The most recent excavation began in June 1976 on a site of about 1500 square metres. The site lay at the centre of Viking York and many interesting finds were made. The water-logged soil, through which the archaeologists dug, preserved objects made of wood, cloth and leather which usually rot away. The excavation at Coppergate presented a rare opportunity to uncover a large area of Viking York. The finds have provided a great deal of information about the Viking settlers.

24 Excavation at Viking York 2

An archaeologist working on timbers at Coppergate

1 What is the archaeologist doing? The text below tells you why.
2 Suggest what happened to the wooden wall on the right-hand side of the building.
3 Use the clues below to say what you think the timber buildings were probably used for. Give reasons for your answer.

The timber buildings at Coppergate

The archaeologists began to uncover a series of most exciting finds in the summer of 1976. They found the remains of three oak buildings. They dug carefully and discovered timber walls two metres high in places. The wood had been preserved by the wet soil although there were signs of woodworm. The archaeologists were able to date the buildings to about AD 1000 from the objects found in them and from the age of the wood. These were the best-preserved Viking timber buildings ever found in Britain. The summer was very hot and the delicate timbers had to be kept damp to stop them crumbling.

Using the clues

The archaeologists set about deciding what the buildings would have looked like in Viking times. An artist's impression of the buildings as they might have been is shown opposite. They had also to consider what the buildings were used for. Here are some of the clues:

1 The site was situated in Coppergate, which means the 'street of the woodworkers'.
2 Domestic utensils and bones of domestic animals were not found.
3 Many wood shavings and pieces of wood were uncovered from the floor of the timber buildings.

A modern artist's reconstruction of the timber buildings at Coppergate, York

4 In what ways does the artist's picture help you to understand more about the timber buildings?
5 Explain how the boot (below) was fastened.
6 History books often suggest that Vikings were simply plunderers and destroyers. How far do you think the finds at Coppergate give us a different picture of the Vikings?
7 What abilities do you think you need to be a successful archaeologist?

The dig

The excavation was one of the most important ever undertaken in Britain. The large site lay in the part of York where in Viking times the making of goods and trading took place. The most up-to-date archaeological methods were used and the objects that had lain in the soil for so long were uncovered with great care. The finds included objects like beads, carved stones and pottery as well as those shown here. The excavation has helped historians to know more about York and to appreciate more fully the way of life of the Vikings.

A leather boot found at Coppergate

25 One kingdom

England becomes one kingdom
The Kings of Wessex, 901-79

901	In this year King Alfred died. Then Edward, his son, succeeded to the kingdom.
924	In this year King Edward passed away and Athelstan, his son, came to the throne.
940	In this year King Athelstan passed away and Edmund, his brother, succeeded to the throne.
946	In this year King Edmund passed away and was succeeded by his brother Prince Eadred.
955	In this year King Eadred passed away and Eadwig, son of Edmund, succeeded to the throne.
959	In this year King Eadwig passed away and was succeeded by Edgar, his brother.
975	In this year Edward, Edgar's son succeeded to the throne.
979	In this year King Edward was murdered and Ethelred, his brother, came to the throne.

from the Anglo-Saxon Chronicle

1 Make a family tree for the kings of Wessex of AD 901-79 (Openings 14 and 17 show how family trees are drawn).

King Athelstan gives a book, Bede's Life of St Cuthbert, *to the monastery in Northumbria where the coffin of St Cuthbert was kept*

2 The monk shown in the picture is probably meant to be St Cuthbert (AD 634-87). Did King Athelstan really meet St Cuthbert?

The royal family of Wessex
The Wessex royal family was a remarkable one. Although King Alfred was the only king of England to be called 'Great', during the next seventy-five years most of the kings who followed him proved worthy successors. The three most important kings were: King Edward, King Athelstan and King Edgar. During their reigns they were kings not only of Wessex but of all England. We have seen how England had seven kings in the seventh century. By the tenth century there was one. England was united under Saxon rulers from the royal house of Wessex.

The kings of Wessex and the church
The later kings of England like King Alfred were helped to rule England by churchmen. It was believed that God had given them the right to rule. In turn, the kings wanted to help the church and to convert heathen people to Christianity. Priests and monks as well as warriors were sent to the Vikings in the Danelaw. The kings gave many gifts to churches and monasteries and encouraged the building of new religious houses. In AD 973 Archbishop Dunstan (see Opening 26) organized a special coronation for King Edgar. This ceremony proclaimed Edgar King of all England.

3 Why do you think the artist wanted to have a likeness of St Cuthbert in the picture?

4 Suggest reasons why King Athelstan gave presents to the monks of this monastery.

A silver penny of King Athelstan, minted in York

5 Write out the inscription (letters) on the coin.

6 Try to identify each of the figures in the picture and say what each is doing.

7 What kind of impression do you think the artist wanted people to have about King Edgar and his gifts?

8 The coin was minted in York. What does this tell you about King Athelstan's power?

A picture taken from a charter: King Edgar gives permission for a new church to be built at Winchester

The reconquest of the Danelaw

King Edward was an experienced warrior and he set out to conquer the Danelaw — the lands where the Vikings had settled in eastern England. The people of Mercia who no longer had a king of their own fought on Edward's side. They were led by his sister Ethelfleda. Gradually the Vikings were defeated and most of them accepted Edward as king. Edward's son Athelstan was also a successful warrior. In AD 937 he won a great battle against a large army of Scots, Britons and Viking invaders in Northumbria. Following this victory Athelstan called himself 'Rex Totius Britanniae' — King of all Britain — on his coins.

King Edgar's coronation

The coronation of Edgar took place when he was thirty years old, after he had ruled for fourteen years. He was now old enough to be made a priest. King Edgar was led into Bath church by two bishops. He removed his crown and lay down before the altar. Then Dunstan raised the king so that he could take the coronation oath. He promised to keep peace and law in his kingdom. Dunstan offered prayers for the king who was annointed with holy oil. He was crowned and blessed. Later King Edgar was rowed on the River Dee by eight lesser kings from Scotland, Cumbria and Wales.

26 St Dunstan

Dunstan writing

Dunstan kneeling before Christ. He may have drawn this picture himself, in about AD 960

1 Make a list of the differences in the way that St Dunstan is shown in each picture.
2 Why do you think St Dunstan has been drawn so small compared with Christ?
3 Why was it important for a churchman like Dunstan to have the support of the king?

St Dunstan's early life

St Dunstan (*c*.909-88) was a famous churchman. He was the son of a Saxon noble and went to school at Glastonbury Abbey in Somerset. It was said that he was 'like a clever bee' and was soon skilled in reading and writing. He also became a fine artist. About 936 he was made a priest at Winchester on the same day as Aethelwold, who became his lifelong friend. King Edward made Dunstan Abbot of Glastonbury about AD 940. Dunstan had the abbey rebuilt and set out firm rules for the monks. However, the new king, Eadwig, quarrelled with Dunstan and sent him away from England in 956.

Dunstan's work

When Edgar became King of England, he invited Dunstan to return to England and appointed him Archbishop of Canterbury in AD 960. Soon Dunstan's friend Oswald was made Bishop of Worcester and Aethelwold became Bishop of Winchester. Many churches had been destroyed by the Vikings and some priests in churches had become lazy. Churches that had fallen into disrepair were restored and some new ones were built. Higher standards of learning and behaviour were expected from priests. Later, in AD 973, Dunstan arranged King Edgar's coronation (see Opening 25).

All Saints Church at Earls Barton, Northamptonshire. Most of the tower was built in the tenth century at the time of St Dunstan. It is 21.3 metres high

Archbishop Dunstan, Bishop Aethelwold and King Edgar hold a scroll on which was written rules for monks

4 Which part of Earls Barton church was added later?
5 Which is King Edgar in the picture? Give reasons for your answer.
6 In the picture what is happening to the monk kneeling below? What is this intended to show?
7 Use the text below to make a timetable of twenty-four hours in the life of a boy in the monastery (AD 1000).
8 Draw a time chart of St Dunstan's life and mark in the main events with dates.

Rules

The three churchmen also built new monasteries and improved the way the monks behaved. Strict rules for monks, called *Regularis Concordia* — 'the agreed code of laws' — were set up. These rules were based on those which St Benedict had written down in the sixth century. Monks were neither to have possessions of their own, nor to marry, and were expected to obey the abbot. A timetable of services, mealtimes and work was established. Monks had to devote themselves to the worship of God and to learning and teaching. These rules are still followed by many monks today.

A day in a monastery, by Aelfric, at Winchester

Master: 'Boy, what did you do today?'

Boy: 'I did many things. This night when I heard the bell, I got up from my bed and went into church and sang Nocturne [2 a.m.] with the monks. After that we sang the service of Matins [daybreak], then Prime [6 a.m.], then Tierce [8 a.m.], and then Mass. After that we sang the service of Sext [11.30 a.m.] and we ate and drank and slept; and we got up to sing Nones [2.30 p.m.] before school.'

Master: 'When will you sing Vespers [6 p.m.] and Compline [8 p.m.]?'

Boy: 'When it is time to.'

27 A Viking King of England

Canute fighting with Edmund Ironside, 1016

Canute was very tall and strong and a very handsome man except that his nose was thin and somewhat crooked and prominent. He had a fair complexion with long fair hair. His eyes were finer and keener than any other man's. He was a great warrior, very valiant and victorious and a man of great luck in everything to do with power.

from the Kyntlinga Saga

1 Describe what is happening in the picture.
2 What is shown on Canute's shield?
3 How far does the likeness of Canute in the picture match the description of him?
4 It is doubtful whether Canute and Edmund ever met in hand-to-hand combat. What do you think the artist was trying to suggest by showing them fighting together?

King Ethelred the Unready (979-1016)

The son of King Edgar, Ethelred, was soon faced with Viking invaders. He was not a brave or determined warrior and did not always receive good advice. King Ethelred paid taxes, or Danegeld, to the Vikings in return for peace. This encouraged the Vikings to come more often and to demand larger Danegelds. In 1002 King Ethelred, in despair and rage, ordered all the Vikings living in England outside the Danelaw to be killed. Among the victims was Gunhild, sister of Swein Forkbeard, the King of Denmark. Her death made Swein determined to conquer England.

King Canute

King Swein was master of England when he died in 1014. His army chose his son, Canute, as king. Some of the English, led by Edmund Ironside, son of Ethelred, fought against Canute but were defeated in 1016. When Edmund died in the same year, Canute, aged twenty, was elected king by the Witan. He soon became a strong and respected ruler. He sent his Viking soldiers back to Denmark after collecting an enormous Danegeld to pay them. There were no Viking invasions during his reign. He brought peace and firm government to England after the fighting of the previous thirty years.

*King Canute and his queen
are shown giving a gift to the
new church at Winchester*

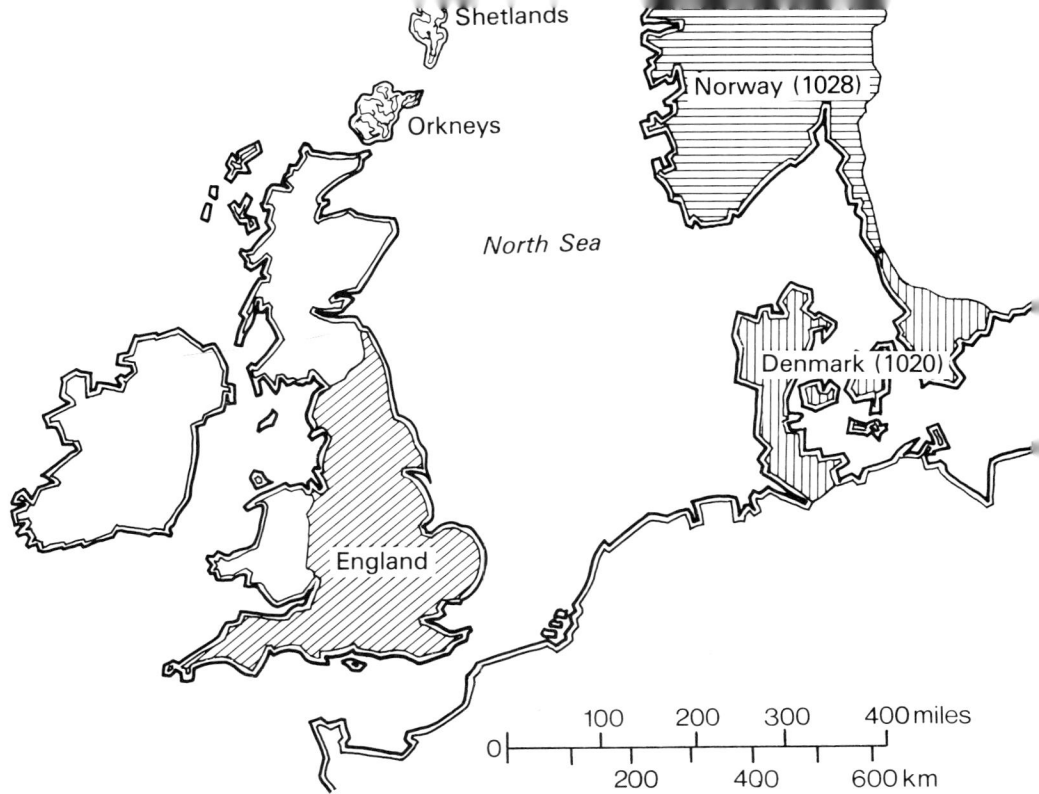

Map of King Canute's empire in 1028

The lands ruled by King Canute

Country	King	What happened to him	Date
England			
		He died	
	King Olaf		

5 Try to identify the various figures in the picture
  and list them.
6 What is Canute's gift to the church?

7 Copy out and complete the chart above.
8 Tell the story of King Canute and the waves
  from the point of view of a courtier.

Canute and the waves

King Canute became a Christian and in 1027 he
made a pilgrimage to Rome. He restored the
damaged churches and monasteries and honoured
the memory of King Edmund whom the Vikings
had murdered (see Opening 16). There is a famous
story concerning King Canute. It is said that
people were always flattering him. One day a
courtier said to Canute that even the waves of the
sea would obey him. So Canute and his courtiers
went down to the sea. Canute sat on his throne
and ordered the waves not to wet him. Of course
the sea took no notice!

Canute's empire

King Canute was not only King of England, but
also of many other lands. His empire included
Denmark, which became Canute's when his
brother Harald died, and Norway after he had
defeated King Olaf. Many English people
benefited from trade with Canute's lands in
Scandinavia. For example, York became a pros-
perous trading town (see Openings 23 and 24).
The second Viking invasion of England was
different from the first. The first had resulted in
many new people settling in Britain, while the
second brought only a Viking king. After Canute
died, the empire was too big for his sons to rule.

28 The Battle of Hastings

All the illustrations on this opening are from the Bayeux Tapestry
The funeral procession of King Edward the Confessor, approaching Westminster Abbey

The coronation of King Harold

1 How many people are carrying Edward's coffin and what are the two men alongside the coffin doing?
2 What shows that Harold has been made king?
3 What name is given to the archbishop and what is he wearing?

The Bayeux Tapestry

The battle of Hastings was one of the most famous battles in the history of Britain. The story of how Duke William of Normandy invaded England is told by the Bayeux Tapestry. The tapestry was probably made for an important Norman lord, Bishop Odo, from the town of Bayeux in Normandy (which is part of France today). It is likely that it was finished by 1080. It is about 49 centimetres wide and 70 metres long. Its seventy-two pictures, embroidered with woollen thread on linen with sub-titles in Latin, form an enormous picture strip. The tapestry was probably embroidered by English craftswomen.

The rivals for the throne of England

Edward, son of King Ethelred, became King of England in 1042. He was not a strong king. Edward was a very religious man and because he was always confessing his sins he was called 'the Confessor'. When he died in January 1066, he had no son to follow him. Harold, Earl of Wessex, a powerful warrior and a determined man, was elected king by the Witan. He was crowned in Westminster Abbey on the same day that Edward was buried. William of Normandy was angry when he heard the news. He claimed both Edward and Harold had promised him that he would be King of England when Edward died.

Duke William's fleet nearing England

King Harold is killed

4 Imagine you were a Saxon noble in Westminster Abbey in January 1066 when one king was buried and another was crowned. Describe the day's events.
5 Find in the top picture Duke William's own ship which carried a special sign on its mast.
6 What is being carried in the ships?
7 Why was it so important to Duke William that there was a favouring wind as the fleet crossed the channel?
8 Historians are not sure whether King Harold is the figure in the tapestry with an arrow in the eye. What do you think? Give reasons for your answer.
9 Describe the Battle of Hastings from the point of view of a Norman knight or an English soldier who survived the fight.

Before the battle

During the summer months there were preparations on both sides of the Channel. William's men cut down trees to make boats and collected armour, weapons and food. Meanwhile King Harold gathered a large army on the south coast of England. In September he heard that Harald Hardrada, King of Norway, who also wanted to be King of England, had landed on the north-east coast. Harold marched 250 miles north and defeated the invaders near York on 25 September. Then three days later William's fleet landed on the south coast at Pevensey.

The Battle of Hastings

King Harold and his tired soldiers marched back south to face William's army. The king drew up his men on Senlac Hill near Hastings. On 14 October the battle began. The two-handled battle-axes of Harold's bodyguards were deadly weapons at close quarters, so William's archers fired arrows from a safe distance. Time after time the Norman knights galloped up the hill, but were forced to turn back. Then part of the Norman army pretended to retreat. Unwisely some of the English chased after them. Late in the day the Normans broke through, killed Harold and defeated the English.

29 The Normans in England

King William the Conqueror

If anyone wishes to know what sort of man he was . . . then we will write of him even as we who have looked upon him and once lived at his court have perceived him to be. This King William was a very wise man and more splendid and powerful than any previous king. He was gentle to good men that loved God and stern beyond all measure to those who resisted his will. In the same place where God permitted him to conquer England he set up a famous monastery and appointed monks for it . . . . He had nobles put in chains who acted against his will . . . but it is not to be forgotten that he made good peace in the land so that any honest man could travel over the kingdom without injury with his bosom full of gold. Castles he let men build. The king took many marks of gold and many hundred pounds of silver from his subjects. There was not one hide of land [about 120 acres] in England that he did not know who owned it and what it was worth.

from the Anglo-Saxon Chronicle, *1087*

1 Do you think the description of King William in the *Anglo-Saxon Chronicle* is likely to be reliable or not? Give reasons for your answer.

Norman soldiers burning a Saxon house (again from the Bayeux tapestry)

2 What reason does the writer give for William's success in conquering England? Why do you think the writer believed this?
3 Why do you think William made a survey of all the land in England?
4 Write contrasting views of William as a king from the point of view of (a) the Normans; (b) the Saxons.

From duke to king

On Christmas Day 1066 Duke William was crowned King of England. He was determined to be master of the country he had conquered. In 1069 there was a rebellion by Englishmen in the north helped by Viking invaders. King William marched northwards and defeated the rebels. To prevent any further trouble he destroyed the countryside in the north of England. Most villages were burnt to the ground. Animals were slaughtered and stores of food were set on fire. There was no more trouble from the English in the north. For nearly a century the lands that King William had laid waste were like a desert.

Domesday Book, *William's survey of England*

An artist's impression of a Norman motte and bailey castle

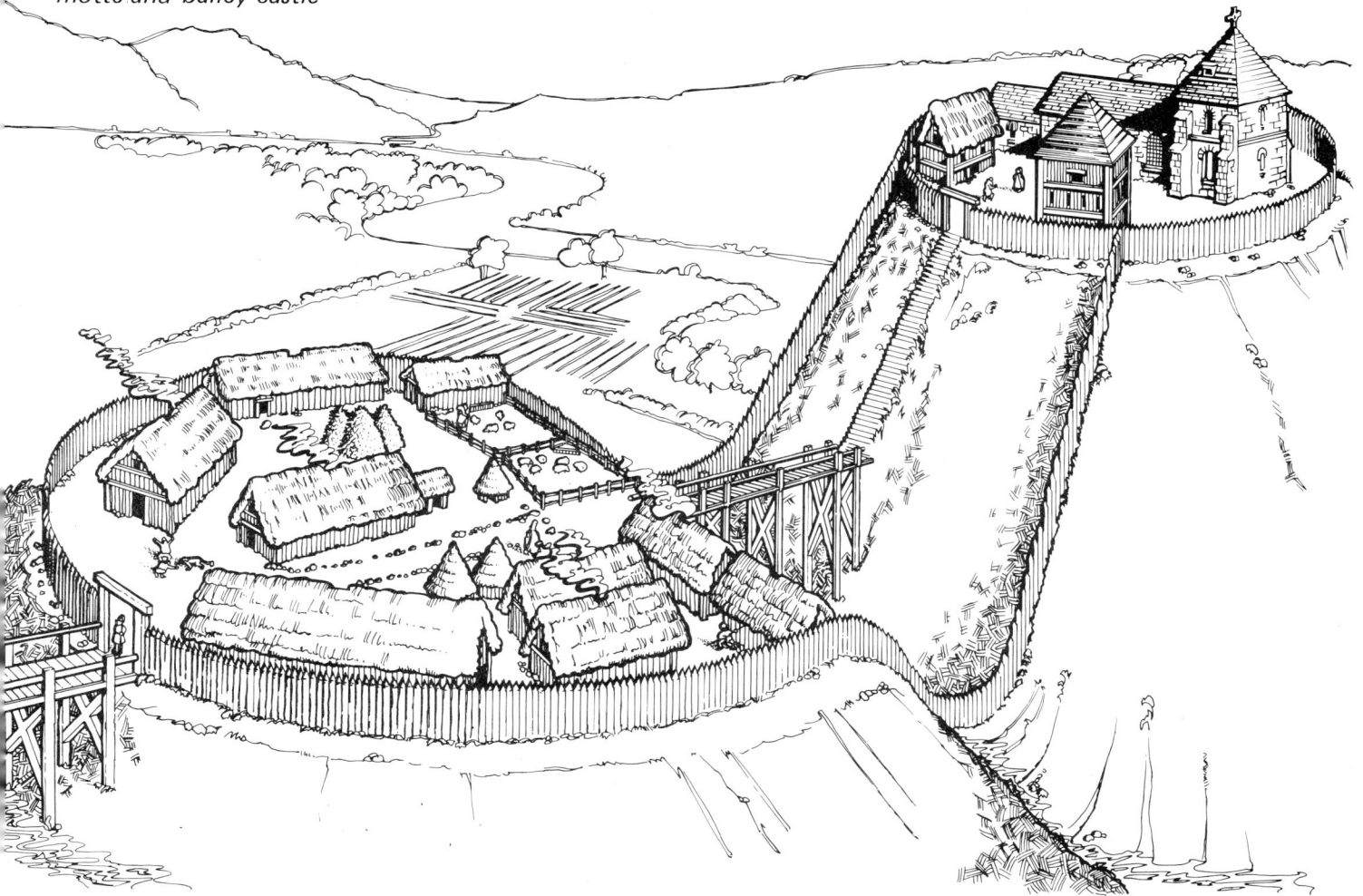

5 Imagine you were a Saxon chief with a group of warriors attacking a Norman motte and bailey castle. Describe all the obstacles you would have to overcome.

6 Draw a cross-section across a motte and bailey castle.

7 Draw a picture strip showing the ways in which William and the Normans became masters of England between 1066 and 1087.

Norman castles

King William took land from the Saxons and gave it to the most important Norman warriors who had helped him conquer England. These men then built strongholds to defend their lands from attack and to control the people. At first these were simple earthworks but soon wooden castles were built on a steep mound (motte) with a fenced enclosure (bailey) surrounded by a moat. Later, stone castles like the White Tower in London were built by the Normans. King William the Conqueror was master of England long before he died in 1087. The last people ever to invade England successfully were now firmly settled.

The White Tower at the Tower of London, completed by 1090

30 Viking Britain 800~1100

AD 800

Alfred, King of
Wessex **871-901**

Edward, King of
England **901-924**

Athelstan, King of
England **924-940**

Edgar, King of
England **959-975**

King Ethelred
979-1016

King Canute
1016-1035

King Edward the
Confessor **1042-1066**

King William 1
1066-1087

900

1000

1100

867

Viking
Kingdom
of York

954

1066   Battle of Hastings

1087   Domesday Book

Viking
raids and
settlement

793   Viking
raid on
Lindisfarne

870   Death of King Edm
of East Anglia

886   Peace between Kir
Alfred and Guthru

960

988

Dunstan, Archbishop
of Canterbury

Second Viking
invasion

Invasions of Britain 400~1100

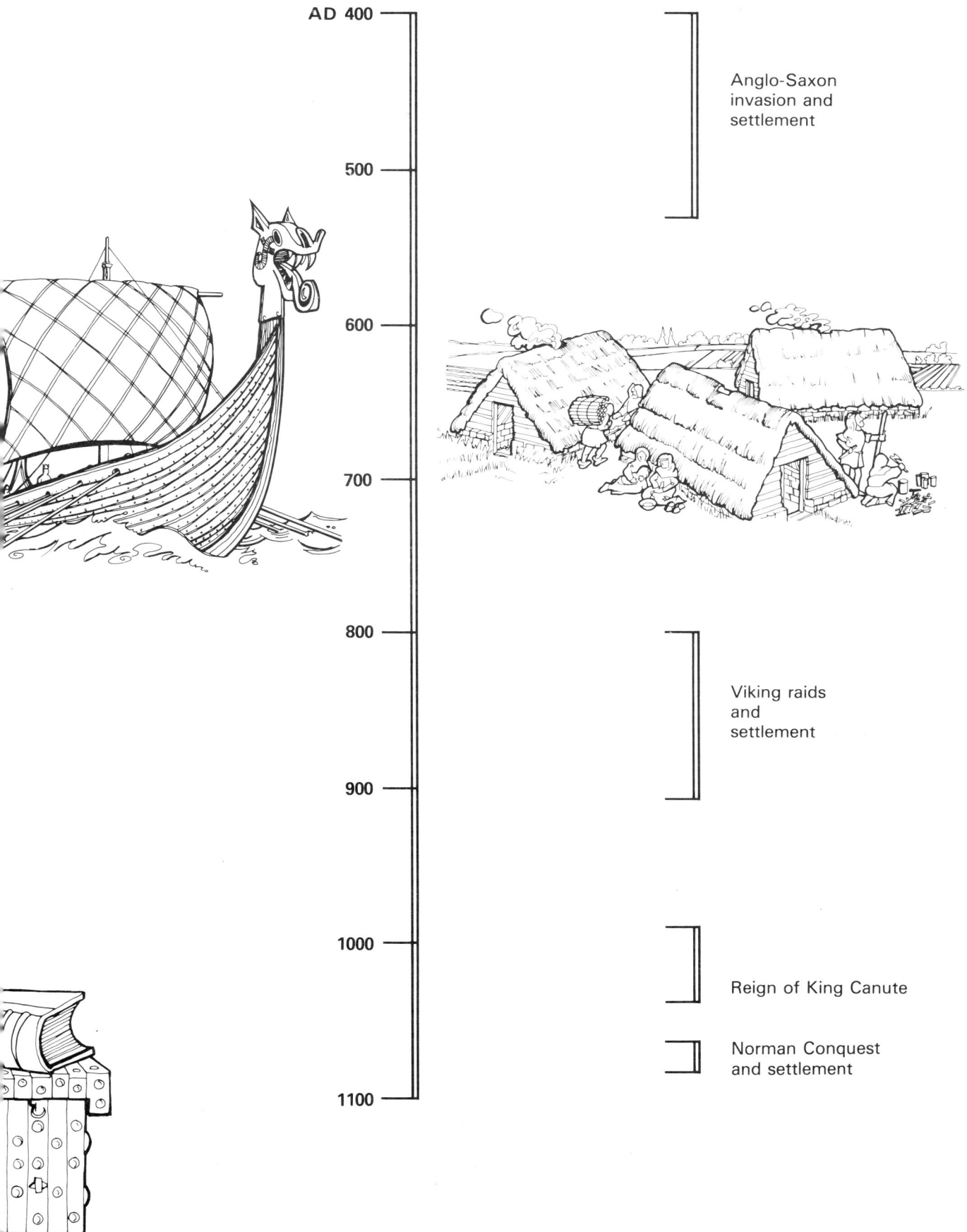

AD 400

Anglo-Saxon
invasion and
settlement

500

600

700

800

Viking raids
and
settlement

900

1000

Reign of King Canute

Norman Conquest
and settlement

1100

Acknowledgements

Every effort has been made to trace owners of copyright material, but in some cases this has not been proved possible. The publisher would be glad to hear from any further copyright owners of material produced in the *Openings in History* series. The author and publisher are grateful to the following for their permission to reproduce illustrations, listed by Opening:

1 boat: Landesmuseum Schleswig-Holsteinisches; carved head: Reproduced by courtesy of the Trustees of the British Museum

2 feast: Mansell Collection; glass tumbler: Reproduced by courtesy of the Trustees of the British Museum

3 calendar and panel: Reproduced by courtesy of the Trustees of the British Museum

4 aerial: Cambridge University Collection, copyright reserved; calendar: Reproduced by courtesy of the Trustees of the British Museum

5 pot: Borough of Ipswich; urn/purse lid/brooch: Reproduced by courtesy of the Trustees of the British Museum; smith: Bodleian Library, Oxford

6 excavation/sceptre/helmet/sword: Reproduced by courtesy of the Trustees of the British Museum

8 Clonmacnois cross/Skellig Michael: Irish National Tourist Office; Ruthwell cross: Department of the Environment, Scotland, Lindisfarne: National Trust

9 wall painting/cross: Reproduced by courtesy of the Dean and Chapter, Durham Cathedral; Farne Island/coffin: Bodleian Library, Oxford

10 Pope: Bibliothèque Nationale, Roger Viollet; font: *Yorkshire Herald*

11 Lindisfarne Gospel: Reproduced by courtesy of the Trustees of the British Museum; Escomb church: A.F. Kersting

12 scribe: Mansell Collection; Bede's History: Reproduced by courtesy of the Trustees of the British Museum

13 woman/hanged man: Reproduced by courtesy of the Trustees of the British Museum

14 Saxon king/penny: Reproduced by courtesy of the Trustees of the British Museum

16 tombstone: Department of the Environment; King Edmund: Pierpoint Morgan Library

17 penny: Reproduced by courtesy of the Trustees of the British Museum; statue: A.F. Kersting

18 statue: A.F. Kersting; jewel: Ashmolean Museum; King David: Reproduced by courtesy of the Trustees of the British Museum

20 longship: Popperfoto; stone: Statens Historiska Museer; reconstructed ship: Universitets Oldsaksamling

21 Gotland Stone/Odin: Statens Historiska Museer; Thor: Iceland National Museum

22 axehead: Copenhagen National Museum; shield/sword/spearhead: Universitets Oldsaksamling; helmet: Statens Historiska Museer; chess-piece: National Museum of Antiquities of Scotland; battle: Reproduced by courtesy of the Trustees of the British Museum

23 view/comb/skate: York Archaeological Trust

24 timber building/boot/reconstruction: York Archaeological Trust

25 Athelstan presents book: Reproduced by courtesy of the Master and Fellows, Corpus Christi College, Cambridge, and the Courtauld Institute of Art, London; Athelstan penny/Edgar and the Almighty: Reproduced by courtesy of the Trustees of the British Museum

26 Dunstan kneels: Bodleian Library, Oxford; Dunstan writing: Radio Times Hulton Picture Library; church: Crown copyright, National Monuments Record; Dunstan/Aethelwold/Edgar: Reproduced by courtesy of the Trustees of the British Museum

27 Canute versus Ironside: Reproduced by courtesy of the Master and Fellows, Corpus Christi College, Cambridge, and the Courtauld Institute of Art, London; Canute as benefactor: Reproduced by courtesy of the Trustees of the British Museum

28 funeral/coronation/fleet/King Harold: Phaidon Press and the Victoria and Albert Museum

29 Norman soldiers: Phaidon Press and the Victoria and Albert Museum; Domesday Book: Public Records Office; White Tower: Department of the Environment

All drawings by Peter Holloway